ACTION SOCIOLOGY AND DEVELOPMENT

ACTION SOCIOLOGY AND DEVELOPMENT

BINDESHWAR PATHAK
Editor

CONCEPT PUBLISHING COMPANY, NEW DELHI 110059

ISBN 81-7022-319-9

First Published 1992

Published and Printed by
Ashok Kumar Mittal
Concept Publishing Company
A/15-16, Commercial Block, Mohan Garden
NEW DELHI 110059 (India)

Lasertypeset by
Microtech Advance Printing Systems (Pvt.) Ltd.
H-13, Bali Nagar,
NEW DELHI 110015

PREFACE

This book owes its origin to the first 'National Seminar on Action Sociology in India' held under the joint auspices of the Sulabh International and the Department of Sociology, Patna University in July 1986. The intention was to initiate a dialogue for conceptual clarity and issue articulation so as to strengthen the foundation of Action Sociology in India. Distinguished social scientists and social activists from the different parts of the country evinced keen interests in the deliberations of the Seminar. In order to consolidate the fruits of the pioneering excercise in this nascent field of scholarship, a need was felt to publish the important articles presented at the Seminar. Subsequently in a bid to make the volume more comprehensive and relevant articles of a few reputed scholars were invited for incorporation. In addition to these, papers containing reflections of experts and specialists, on social dimensions of low cost sanitation, presented at two prestigious seminars conducted in collaboration with the Sulabh International have also been included.

I am particularly beholden to the contributors who through their writings have provided valuable insights on a theme deserving immediate attention of Sociologists. I am grateful to Prof. Z. Ahmad, Professor and Head, Department of Sociology Patna University for his scholarly support in my endeavour to hold the seminar on Action Sociology. Dr. A.K. Lal, Director Sulabh Centre for Action Sociology, New Delhi, has helped in making this publication possible. He provided assistance at various stages. I am thankful to him. My sincere thanks are due to Sri Ashok Kumar Mittal of the Concept Publishing Company, New Delhi for having agreed to publish the book in such a short time.

BINDESHWAR PATHAK
Founder, Sulabh International
Chairman, Sulabh Foundation
Chairman, Indian Association of Action Sociologists

New Delhi

CONTENTS

Preface v
Contributors ix

I. THE THEME

Keynote Address 3
– *Bindeshwar Pathak*
Introduction 7
– *Bindeshwar Pathak*

II. ACTION SOCIOLOGY

1: Action Research in Sociology 15
– *Sachchidananda*
2. Action Sociology and Rural Development 26
– *N.C. Choudhury*
3. Action Sociology : Some Reflections 35
– *Jose Kananaikil*
4. The Need for Action Sociology 42
– *A.K. Lal*
5. Nature, Scope and Suggested Contents of the Postgraduate Course on 'Action Sociology' 47
– *A.D. Singh*

III. NEED FOR SOCIAL INTERVENTION

6. Continuity Without Change : A Perspective Paper on Education 53
– *Ali Ashraf*
7. The Action Sociology in North-East India 62
– *A.C. Sinha*

8. Planned Social Intervention and its Sociological Prerequisites — 70
– T.N. Valunjkar

9. Women and Shudras : Some Observations — 76
– Archana Sinha and *Nidhi Sinha*

10. Caste Conflict and Violence — 81
– M.Z. Khan

11. Challenge of Development, Sociology and Action Sociologist — 96
– S.N. Tiwari

12. Action Sociologists and Development : Some Case Studies — 100
– Manohar Lal

13. Action Sociologist : Voluntary Organizations and Development (A Case Study of Samanwaya Vidyapeeth, Bagha) — 105
– Anirudha Prasad

14. Child Development : An Area for Action Sociology — 110
– B.B. Mandal

15. Action Sociology, Bureaucracy and Voluntary Agencies — 116
– Nil Ratan

IV. SOCIAL DIMENSIONS OF LOW COST SANITATION

16. The Sulabh Movement — 125
– Bindeshwar Pathak

17. Rehabilitation of Liberated Scavengers — 128
– B.N. Srivastava

18. Low Cost Sanitation in Tamil Nadu: Social Aspects — 139
– Paul P. Appasamy and *D. Sundaram*

19. Low Cost Sanitation Project in Tamil Nadu: Social Aspects — 151
– N. Athimoolam

20. Sociological Approach to Evaluation of Community Toilet Complexes — 157
– Sachchidananda

21. Low Cost Sanitation — Organization, Training and Extension — 160
– A.K. Lal

CONTRIBUTORS

DR. BINDESHWAR PATHAK, Padma Bhushan
Founder, Sulabh International, Patna.

DR. SACHCHIDANANDA
Professor Emeritus, A.N. Sinha Institute of Social Studies, Patna-1

DR. ALI ASHRAF
Director, Gandhian Institute of Studies, Varanasi-1

SHRI B.N. SRIVASTAVA
Director, Department of Welfare, Ministry of Home Affairs, New Delhi.

PROF. A.D. SINGH
Management Consultant, Jamshedpur.

DR. N.C. CHOUDHURY
Former Professor of Sociology, Department of Sociology and Social Anthropology, University of North Bengal.

DR. T.N. VALUNJKAR
Former Professor of Sociology, University of Poona, Poona.

DR. M.Z. KHAN
Professor of Social Work, Jamia Millia Islamia, New Delhi.

DR. D. SUNDARAM
Professor and Head, Department of Sociology, University of Madras, Madras

DR. A.K. LAL
Director, Sulabh Centre for Action Sociology, New Delhi-45.

DR. A.C. SINHA
Professor and Head of the Department of Sociology, North-Eastern Hill University, Shillong.

SHRI N. ATHIMOOLAM
Labour Commissioner, Government of Tamil Nadu.

DR. ARCHANA SINHA
Professor and Head of the Department of Sociology, M.M. College, Patna University, Patna.

DR. JOSE KANANAIKIL
Indian Social Institute, New Delhi.

DR. B.B. MANDAL

Reader in Sociology and Social Anthropology, A.N. Sinha Institute of Social Studies, Patna.

DR. S.N. TIWARI

Reader in Sociology, L.N. Mithila University, Darbhanga (Bihar).

DR. MANOHAR LAL

Department of Sociology A.N. Sinha Institute of Social Studies, Patna.

DR. ANIRUDHA PRASAD

General Manager, District Industries, Muzafarpur.

DR. NIL RATAN

Department of Political Science and Public Administration, A.N. Sinha Institute of Social Studies, Patna.

DR. PAUL P. APPASAMY

Visiting Fellow, Madras Institute of Development Studies Madras

NIDHI SINHA

Research Fellow, Department of Sociology, Patna University, Patna.

I

THE THEME

KEYNOTE ADDRESS*

BINDESHWAR PATHAK

I am exceedingly delighted to be with you today and to participate in the deliberations of this seminar on "Action Sociology in India". I am thankful to you for the honour you have in your overflowing affection done me by asking me to present the Keynote Address before this gathering of distinguished scholars, all of whom are well known for their insight wisdom and enviable erudition.

Before the back-breaking burden of presenting the Keynote Address was placed on my shoulders, the names of some of the most celebrated sociologists of India were discussed and considered by the organizers of this Seminar, but they resolved, to my bewilderment, that I, and none else, should deliver this Address, for I am, they said, the initiator of the idea of Action Sociology. Their argument was so appealingly clothed in reason's garb that I had to submit to their will, for who can dispute that the originator of an idea must first explain what its essential ingredients are, what in reality it symbolizes or what it means. While the organizers looked upon me as a trail-blazor, I regarded myself as a dwarf, a Lilliputian, a manikin facing a resplendent galaxy of so many literary Brobdingnagians and eminent sociologists. Realizing that even small fries are sometimes in the saddle, I accepted this onerous responsibility and am, therefore, before you with my Address.

I must admit, ladies and gentlemen, that I do not possess that erudition or that expertise which sociologists of your eminence possess. All that I know is mostly derived from the practical experiences of life, of actions performed and their fruits reaped. I would, therefore, humbly submit that if there be any slips and omissions in my address, you will in your profound wisdom ignore them.

* Delivered at the First National Seminar on Action Sociology in India, Patna, 28th July 1986.

Before I try to highlight the aims and objectives of the Seminar, a few words about my involvement in this programme will not be out of place here, for they would enable you to glimpse the underlying unity between my life, my works, my attainments, and this Action Sociological Seminar, and to ascertain whether my experiences can be cherished or rejected by my contemporaries or my successors. If what I have experienced is to be valued and if attainments in my field of endeavour are to be prized, will some modifications be necessary? If yes, to what extent and in what form ?

One of the missions of my life was to be a lecturer in Sociology, a dream that has remained unrealized to this day. Although I had a brilliant academic career, yet due to some reasons beyond my comprehensions, I could not get a first class from Patna University in 1964 at the graduate level, and this led to my abandonment of post-graduate studies and acceptance of the life of a tireless wanderer roaming from one place to another, searching for an occupation which could bring me a degree or a measure of job satisfaction. I was, however, compelled by circumstances to start my career as a school teacher in a high school, then to switch my energies on to the Electricity Board, Bihar, and again to engage myself in the business of medicines and finally to the Bihar Gandhi Centenary Celebration Committee in 1967 where I came to have a first-hand acquaintance with the philosophy of Mahatma Gandhi with its accent on the liberation of scavengers from the demeaning practice of carrying human excreta, and on their rehabilitation in other occupations. Just as Mahatma Gandhi got the idea of honouring and speaking the truth after seeing the famous "Harishchandra Natak", so did I stumble upon the idea of doing away with the sub-human system of carrying human excreta during the Gandhi Centenary period. The programme of the liberation of scavengers has kept me engaged right up to this day and has brought me some laurels too. I have also been able to develop some such concepts as construction and maintenance of public conveniences on pay-and-use basis, production of biogas from human excreta and its conversion into energy, provision of sanitary latrines and smokeless *chullah* in rural areas, afforestation, maintenance of hand-pumps, family welfare schemes, adult education, etc. Experiences, so rich and varied, helped me apply sociological theories to social needs, translate these theories into practice and reap a rich harvest of useful results.

The spiritual urge to liberate the scavengers and to be increasingly responsive to the nation in general and contemporary society in particular led me to embark upon a voyage of discovery, discovery of the possibility of teaching topics like sanitary latrines, biogas, smokeless *chullah*, maintenance of hand-pumps, adult education, housing, family welfare, afforestation, cottage industries, etc., at the post-graduate level and later on at all levels from school up to college so that our boys could learn about these programmes, and how they are being implemented in the villages where they shall have to go back to accelerate the pace of rural development. If they are taught these subjects as an integral part of their curriculum, it would enable them to secure self-employment and end that abject poverty which plagues our society today. Apart from these obvious advantages, they will help in building up the nation and in serving the rural people, who constitute 80 per cent of the Indian population.

If scholarly investigation and research have to be harnessed and made to serve the teeming millions of our country, they must not remain confined to theoretical explication and analysis, however suitable and profound they may be. The research must be sent to rural areas and work at the Block or the Panchayat level and render all possible help to the process of rural development, rectifying its defects, if any, and recording his experiences of rural life from the day he goes there to the day of his return. The investigator preparing for the Master's degree or for a Doctorate must also explain how he got the errors rectified, which would enable other students to derive whatever benefits they can from his experiences. This will also enable our students to be self-reliant and cease to be a burden on the resources of the country.

When I expressed my feelings in this regard to Dr. Z. Ahmad, Professor and Head of the Department of Sociology, Patna University, and hinted at the possibility of teaching these topics at the post-graduate level and gradually at the grassroot level too, my learned guide, who had supervised my doctoral thesis on sociology, approved of my idea, but added at the same time that I should obtain the national consensus on the subject. With this end in view, we organized a "State Level Workshop" on June 20, 1986, which to our great pleasure was attended by such eminent celebrities as Prof. I.S. Chauhan from Bhopal University and Dr. M.Z. Khan, from Jamia Millia University. This workshop made some historic recommendations, including the one that a "National Seminar" be convened before the World Congress of Sociology" scheduled to be held in Delhi sometime in August, 1986, and the recommendations of the "National Level Workshop" be sent to the "World Congress" for due consideration and endorsement. I would like to appeal to all the participants, distinguished in this field for their well-knownness and vast, scholarship, especially to Prof. C. Lakshmanna, President of this inaugural session to persuade the organizers of the "World Congress" to discuss this issue there and to make sociology more action-oriented; more practical and more salutary to mankind. I assure you, ladies and gentlemen, that I will be available for further discussion on this issue during the deliberations of this seminar and would love to elaborate the topic to your heart's content. I am not expatiating on this matter at present due to paucity of time, but suffice it to say that the Vocational Training Programmes, which have been glibly talked about and discussed at various levels, lay considerable stress on the significance of Action Sociology, for it is no secret by now that no programme will have its full fruition if it is not based upon correct and in-depth knowledge of social taboos and totems. The new Education Policy, generally labelled "The National Policy on Education", accords due recognition to Action Programmes and underscores the necessity of a thorough knowledge of the socio-culture of Indian national life. At one of the meetings of the National Development Council held on April 29, 1986, the Late Prime Minister of India, Shri Rajiv Gandhi, not only expounded the National Policy on Education but also laid stress on understanding human nature and social life, declaring, "The new policy is an attempt to re-link learning with life as it is in India, whether in the rural areas or in the tribal areas, whether in the hills or in the mountains or in the forests." Obviously the National Policy on Education is a policy inextricably rooted in Action Programmes. I am sure, then that the New Policy will be crowned with success, for it is not confined to the ideological level alone but is wedded to action and to the implementation of action on the basis of extensive as well as intensive knowledge of socio-cultural values and conditions. I will, therefore, conclude this Address with the observation that the National Policy on Education and Action Sociology have consented to be joined together in holy wedlock, as it were, and pledged truth to each other.

I am thankful to all of you, honourable Sirs, for giving me a patient hearing, for which gracious compassion and your love of learning, I wish the Seminar a grand success.

INTRODUCTION

BINDESHWAR PATHAK

Action Sociology is action-oriented proxeological sociology. It aims at Sociologist's intervention to shape the process of social change. Action sociologists have to contribute to the solution of the problems of society by directly involving themselves. Sociology, in spite of the strides it has made in unravelling the complex social realities, tends to remain, by and large, indifferent to their roles as effective agents to guide the direction of change. Instead of actively involving in this endeavour, they have remained a mute witness to the existing as well as emerging social realities. Structuring the conceptual and methodological paradigms to interpret the phenomenon under study, however, seems to be an academic luxury, in the wake of the existence of issues seeking the urgent intervention of sociologists for the solution. Linking of scientific knowledge with social issues, is not all that society expects from Sociologists. The accumulation of vast literature gathered through the empirical studies may help in interpreting the directionalities of social change. But these fall short of the expectations. These may provide sound feedbacks to the administrators and agencies entrusted with the task of implementing programmes for development. However, in order to receive an expert treatment the enormous problems confronting the society requires the effective involvement of Sociologists. Action sociologists have to activate strategies for developing society. There is an urgent need to identify priority areas and appropriate strategies to steer the process of change in the desired direction. The gap between knowledge and practice has to be bridged with the sustained involvement in the process of development. Action sociology, it may be noted, is an innovative field, and not a fashionable addition to the enlarging horizons of sociology. It protects Sociology against insulating scholarship from practice. Sociology has to extricate itself from the maze of concepts and theories become action-oriented to be a practical instrument for social change. Action sociology emphasizes reconstruction of society so as to protect it against the forces of stagnation and exploitation. It requires sustained efforts from dedicated Sociologists to effectively encounter the inherent aberrations of an inegalitarian social structure in need of radical transformation. Sociologists' indifference towards the urgent problems of society has to end for the survival of the discipline.

Since Action Sociology is a new concept that emerged out of my encounter with the problems of scavengers, I felt the need to initiate a dialogue among the sociologists to arrive at clarifications and issue articulation to strengthen the foundation of the new discipline. A National Seminar was held towards this end under the joint sponsorship of Sulabh International and Department of Sociology, Patna University, from July 28 to 30, 1986 at Patna. This volume represents a collection of select articles presented at the seminar. These, read together, provide glimpses into the responses of the Sociologists assembled on the occasion to the concept of and issues involved in Action Sociology. Some articles have been provided to us by the authors on our special request to make the volume more comprehensive. Some papers highlight the action-oriented sociological programmes in the field of sanitation and problems of scavenging. These were presented at seminar organized by the Sulabh International at different places.

II

Professor Sachchidananda in his paper rejects the conceptualization of action research as an application of existing theory to some practical problems. He considers participatory research to be the confluence of theory, research and practice. It involves dialogue between actors and researchers. This is also called discourse-oriented research. In this the actor plays the dominant role of orientating the activities of researchers for specific purposes. The researcher helps the actors in articulating their orientations through a process of continued dialogue. Participatory discourse, he feels, being complicated, requires personal discipline on the part of researcher in order to keep his identity intact. It emphasizes the actor's role as creator of society using manipulative and processual consciousness produced as premises for inquiry and discourse. Action research, he emphasises, is characterized by interlocking between cultural factors, action and basic structures and processes. Action research is attuned to the practical concerns of the people. It is a type of applied research with overriding emphasis on researcher's involvement in the action process for organizational change. Its tentative, non-committed and adaptive character makes it differ from summative evaluation. He emphasizes the need for utilizing the immense good work done by the research organizations of the country to find out the workable solution of the existing problems.

Prof. N.C. Choudhury in his paper "Action Sociology and Rural Development" congratulates the Sociologists for their contributions towards understanding the texture of society. This has been made possible through the excellent studies on the urgent problems of sociological research. There, now, exists an accumulation of vast literature to help them identify priority areas for deeper involvement. The author feels that Action Sociology has to concern itself with ensuring the involvement of Sociologists in all stages of development. The roots of the social problems have to be identified to suggest remedial measures involving deep and active association of Sociologists in planning, execution, monitoring and evaluation of the programmes designed to solve the problem. This in term requires radical modification of the curricula of teaching of sociology so as to inculcate among the students the needed instinct, drive and skill for associating themselves with the execution of development programmes of the country.

Dr. Jose Kananaikil in his paper "Action Sociology : Some Reflections" feels a need for systematic study of the problems of the people in order to identify suitable action programmes to contain them. Action Sociology is the need of the hour, it is neither a luxury, nor a fad. Sociologists rooted in the life experiences of the people having courage to respond to the various social problems and possessing intellectual capacity to build new models are needed to strengthen the field of Action Sociology.

Dr. A.K. Lal in his paper "The Need for Action Sociology" pleads for a radical reorientation in the working tradition of Sociology so as to make it useful for society. Attempts have to be made to use sociological findings for effective and sustained development. Intervention in the process of change has to be the primary responsibility of the Sociologists. Action Sociology, he asserts, is poised to emerge as a major contemporary influence to take up the issues afflicting society. Sociologists have to be the catalysts completely involved in the process of change. This success of Sulabh International in effectively encountering the problems of society, under the leadership of an Action Sociologists, bears testimony to the tremendous potentiality of this discipline in solving the problems of society. The author provides a list of priority areas seeking immediate attention of Action Sociologists.

Prof. A.D. Singh insists upon having practical training for the Sociologists on the completion of their education in the University. He feels that Sociologists have lagged behind in acquiring skills that could help the experts in solving the problems of society. There is a need on the part of sociologists to get them acquainted with the technological innovations having the potentiality to affect the web of social relations. His paper includes course contents that have to be adopted by the Universities for preparing Action Sociologists.

III

The next set of papers contain analysis of cases that have received or are seeking involvement of Action Sociologists for effective implementation. Thus Prof. Ali Ashraf in his paper "Continuing Without Change" feels the need for sincere efforts to research the educational system to make it responsive to the actual needs of society. This, he feels, has to be urgently attended to ensure rapid socio-economic development. Problems afflicting the Indian society have assumed alarming proportions in the absence of teaching aimed at inculcation of appropriate values of modernization. Education has to be an instrument of nation-building and socio-economic development. It has to be attained to the needs and aspirations of the people. This can be attained with the help of institutions wedded to the goal of preparing people for sectors that remain undeveloped in the absence of skilled personnel. Expensive centres of education have produced elites who remain indifferent to the problems at the grassroot. Education has to be closely linked with realistic programmes of economic development and social reforms as a long-term strategy to solve the twin problems of unemployment and socio-economic development. Incidentally it may have to be noted in tune with this line of thinking that Sulabh International on its own has initiated a training programme for integrated rural development by providing training to the jobless in such skills as have the potential of bridging the gap between education and requirements of development.

Prof. A.C. Sinha in his paper "The Action Sociology in North-East India" presents a portrait of the contours of social life in North-East India. As a keen observer of the pattern of change that is affecting the prevalent egalitarian set-up characterizing that area, he stresses the need for action-oriented sociological intervention to stop the exploitation of scavengers, which is of recent origin.

Prof. T.N. Valunjkar in his paper "Planned Social Intervention and its Sociological Prerequisites" calls upon the voluntary organizations to play an active role for achievement of the social goals enshrined in our Constitution. The action programmes for accomplishment of these and some other goals have to be drafted after taking into consideration the structural context of the milieu. Action programmes for social change, have to emphasize resocialization and conscientization of the disadvantaged so that initiation of efforts for change may acquire bottom up direction.

Prof. Archana Sinha and Ms Nidhi Sinha have great expectations from Action Sociologists in improving the status of women and untouchables. They describe the status of untouchables as that of a community slaves in traditional India. Their abject subordination to the caste Hindus acquired legitimacy for the religious texts. Under the British these people remained condemned to the low status accorded to them by society. They occupied houses on the outskirts of the towns and villages. In independent India their accumulated anger found manifestation in their aggressive and concerted efforts to counter the perpetuation of exploitation. This needs to be tackled by Action Sociologists by building up a harmonious and egalitarian social structure.

Violence as manifested in the incidents of caste conflict represents an area seeking intervention of Action Sociologists to rid the country from a situation of anarchy and chaos. Prof. M.Z. Khan in his paper "Caste Conflict and Violence" considers ascription-oriented hierarchy as the most distinctive feature of Indian society. The inequalities thus institutionalized by tradition have all the makings of a conflict situation. The inegalitarian social structure legitimized the exploitation of those at the bottom of the caste hierarchy at times through coercive measures. The contemporary setting characterized by changed socio-economic and political spectrum upset the traditional elite and have led to conflicts between the traditionally privileged castes and new status asserting groups. Prof. Khan in his paper examines in detail the incidents of caste violence to uncover the causes underlying them.

In rural areas caste remains entrenched in spite of the forces of a change. The evidences documented in the paper do not corroborate the postulation that caste conflicts in village India necessarily represent class conflict in a transformed or underdeveloped form.

Dr. S.N. Tiwari emphasizes the need for investigating the problems of poverty and underdevelopment in detail. Such studies have to be followed by active involvement of the Sociologists in building up a mass awareness programme among these people. Social education of the recipients of the delivery system has to be through the expert involvement of the Sociologists. In fact through these activities only the Sociologists can find a place of relevance in society.

Dr. Manohar Lal in his article "Action Sociologists and Development" emphasises the role of the Action Sociologists, as advisers, Consultants and expert designers of projects, with a sociological bias. His experience of participatory involvement in the programmes for rural development leads him to conclude that through participatory intervention Action Sociologists may help in identification of barriers to people's participation in development programmes and evaluation of the ongoing schemes of development.

Dr. Anirudha Prasad in his paper "Action Sociologists: Voluntary Organizations and Development" describes the efforts of a voluntary organization in Bihar devoted to the cause of upliftment of Mushahars — a scheduled caste placed at the rock bottom of the socio-economic hierarchy. The problems encountered by the organization not only from the entrenched in the village but also from the target group itself finds detailed elaboration. The most important contribution of the voluntary organization has been to wean the Mushahars away from the clutches of bondage.

Dr. B.B. Mandal in his paper "Child Development: An Area for Action Sociology" stresses the need for involvement on the part of Action Sociologists in the field of child care and control. Basing his observation on the field experiences in Bihar he feels that the prevalent infrastructural inadequacy and inefficiency afflicting the State stand a fair chance of rectification through the active involvement of Action Sociologists. He provides a list of prescriptions and guidelines that have to be taken note of by the active interventionists engaged in this field.

Dr. Nil Ratan in his paper "Action Sociology, Bureaucracy and Voluntary Agencies" calls, for an effective blending of expertise and action on the part of social scientists to ensure effective development.

Social scientists he feels, have to work in close collaboration with bureaucratic and voluntary organisations. This is necessary to ensure success in programmes of development.

IV

In the last section we have five papers dealing with social dimensions of the problems of sanitation and scavenging and the role of Sulabh International in solving them. Thus Dr. Pathak in his paper on the Sulabh movement describes his experiences that came in the wake of his encounters with suitable *Shauchalaya* for adoption among the people. Its large-scale adoption to solve the problem of disposal of human excreta in a scientific manner has been possible through adequate understanding of the needs and aspirations of the people. The paper is a detailed and indepth account of the author's contribution towards ushering in a social change of an unprecedented magnitude through much-needed effective social intervention.

Mr. B.N. Srivastava considers scavenging to be a slur in spite of existence of modernized methods of excreta disposal. Provision for sanitary latrines, he feels, have not acquired the dimensions it merits. The author feels that the hand-flush water-seal sanitary latrine is the most effective solution to the problems of sanitation. Elaborating the achievements made in this regard through State efforts, Mr Srivastava pleads for a more concerted campaign in this regard. He also emphasizes the need for the rehabilitation programmes for the scavengers and their sons and daughters. A number of schemes and programmes launched, find elaboration in his paper.

Dr. Paul Appasamy and Dr. Sundaram in their paper "Low Cost Sanitation in Tamil Nadu: Social Aspects" make a plea for incorporation sanitation as a major component in the plan allocation. They feel that the steps taken to solve the sanitary problems of the country have been thoroughly inadequate. Slums and smaller towns, they feel could best get their sanitation problem solved through low-cost sanitation. Among the available technological options, the State has to select that which is appropriate. There is a need for long-term commitment to the goals of sanitation and involvement of the people in the implementation of the programmes meant for them.

Mr. N. Athimoolam in his paper "Seminar on Low Cost Sanitation Project in Tamil Nadu: Social Aspects" describes the role of Tamil Nadu water supply and drainage latrine programmes in Tamil Nadu.

He describes the low-cost technology for excreta disposal to be a technology with human face. His paper encapsulates gleanings of the evaluation reports on low-cost sanitation in the States of Bihar, Tamil Nadu and Gujarat as prepared by the Technology Advisory group. He also pleads the case of having more and more community latrines to cater to the needs of homeless and floating population. The paper contains a few suggestions to ensure the effectiveness of the innovative sanitation programmes. These again have been culled out from the report of the study mentioned above.

Community toilet complex as envisaged by Dr. Bindeshwar Pathak has been described by Prof. Sachchidananda in his paper "Sociological Approach to Evaluation of Community Toilet Complexes" to be quite effective in catering to some of the basic needs of the people. The author feels that there is a need for evaluating the impact of such complexes in altering the orientation of the people not only in the field of sanitation but in ushering in a new phase in their outlook towards life.

Dr. A.K. Lal in his paper "Low Cost Sanitation: Organization, Training and Extension" stresses the need for sustained efforts to ensure widespread diffusion of low-cost sanitation. Approaches to such problems need not be sporadic and casual any longer. He praises the role of an effective delivery system evolved by the Sulabh International for adoption of its technology of excreta disposal. Sanitation, the author concludes, has a better chance of acceptance as a constituent of an integrated programme for development. This in turn requires a comprehensive training for human resource development.

II

ACTION SOCIOLOGY

1

ACTION RESEARCH IN SOCIOLOGY

SACHCHIDANANDA

In the first two development decades (1950-1970) sociologists all the world over were under the spell of the concept of modernization. This was sought to be studied through the diffusion of innovation approach. They were concerned with who accepted the innovations and why as well as with the resistance to change. By the beginning of the 70s, however, modernization was seen by the sociologists from the developing countries as an instrument for increasing new colonial dependency, as a process which accelerated the accumulation of wealth and power among the westernized "progressive" or "dynamic" indigenous elites, increasing class and ethnic cleavages leading to destruction of traditional patterns of social morality and their replacement with highly competitive rush for scarce wealth which could only leave the masses even more deprived than before. People in these countries found it difficult to survive without the supportive social networks.

Faced with this situation, the sociologists broadened the scope of the innovative process to include not only the work needed to spread innovation but also the identification and awareness of the underlying problem to be solved as seen in the perspective of the periphery and the organization of the people who suffer from the people. The innovative process is thus seen involving both an increasing consciousness of grassroot problems and innovative action to solve these problems from below. It was seen that the problem solution coming from the above does not always fit the problem as seen from below. The crucial issue is, therefore, how to define and operationalize, and to deal with the degree of fit between the problems and the problem solutions in the innovative processes of change or transformations.

A further advance in this line of thinking was the stress on methodological bias for participatory action research. However, action research is not conceived in the manner of Kurt Lewin (1948) as an application of the existing theory to some practical problems in a field setting with an instrumental, quasi-experimental design resulting in distinctly separate practical results on the one hand and research reports on the other. Participatory action research is conceived as an inseparable combination of theory, research and practice characterized by a dialogue between actors and researchers about the meaning of the action intended and eventually resulting in an increasing autonomy of actors in relationship to the researchers (Himmelstrand, U. : 1982:44).

This kind of research could also be called discourse-oriented action research.[1] In such research the intentions of action are not given in advance by researchers but by the actors themselves. The role of the researcher is to help clarify the intentions of actors in the context of relevant structural conditions, options and constraints through a process of continued dialogue. The research reports contain analytical descriptive accounts of this process, the action, its constraints and consequences, mistakes made and discovered in this process and fed back to him the understanding of the situation leading to further action. The aim of discourse-oriented action research is to provide people with their own voice as suggested by Paulo Freire rather than to estimate and report success of experimental manipulation in the field setting.

The steps involved in discourse-oriented action research start with information gathering in the context of action. Relevant information refers to the stock of local and everyday knowledge, knowledge of local history, local institutions, rules, current events processed by local actors. The knowledge about the wider structural contexts of province, national and international dependencies may also be crucial for understanding the nature of the predicaments which conscientization and action is all about. Information has to be gathered about antagonists also with whom discourse is difficult. In the second stage, the contextual information obtained in the first stage is used as a context for discussion argumentation and clarification between actors and researchers. The aim is to arrive at an enlightened consciousness among the actors about the nature of the situation and on the action to be taken up. Then follows the stage of social action. This often involves mistakes, ruptures and unexpected consequences on which information must be assembled for the sake of further action and research and feedback to a revised assessment of the context and the manner of action.

The entire process of participatory discourse-oriented action research is difficult and complicated. Even if there are no dangers of persecution and oppression from established authorities there are two internal problems. It has to be noted that the action has to be location specific and it will take precedence over the universalistic requirements of research. Such problems arise in other kinds of research also but in this particular kind of research due to the close identification of the researchers with the actors, the problems become all the more difficult. The second problem is when the researcher becomes strongly committed with the actors. The researcher must avoid becoming so identified and involved with the actors that he relinquishes his autonomy as a researcher. The researcher in this kind of research should take on the role of the actor but refuse to identify with the standpoint of the actor. This, of course, requires a great deal of personal discipline. There can be some problems at the actor level too. It has to be seen that the basic preconditions of true dialogue between actors and researchers is not disrupted. It is necessary that a preliminary analysis of antagonistic and non-antagonistic conflict of interest in the area of action must precede the initiation of a participatory discourse-oriented research project.

Social sciences have been preoccupied for a long time with tackling the problems of causal explanation leaving the domain of human intercourse almost unexplored. Their methodology is not developed to deal with this latter domain. Till now social scientists were studying people as products of society not as creators of society. Social science paradigms help us understand how we are created by society but not how we create society. Both the domains are legitimate areas of scientific analysis but the area most neglected needs more attention at present. Since manipulative and processual consciousness production is a fact of life, it must be studied as such but the consciousness produced and studies in such a manner could be seen not as baselines for further manipulative or processual consciousness production but as premises for enquiry and discourse among actors becoming involved in a project of emancipation and self-managed change. Such action projects require a different research methodology. These different methods are not less scientific in character than methods geared to casual manipulation.

The theories on modes of construction of society by man must start not from the reconstruction of mythical natural condition but from an understanding of contemporary society as given point of departure for the construction of the future. Such construction involves struggle with an uncertain outcome among the actors with diverse and even contradictory interests, contradictions produced by given social structure and resolvable by structural transformations, that is, by rational re-arrangements of structural elements.

In action research there is intricate interlocking of three domains of knowledge namely cultural factors, fields of action and basic structures and processes. Cultural factors include stocks of designs, ideas, normative standards and organizational forms. These interact with processes of consciousness and more or less innovative struggle. Interaction between all these affects actors such as individuals, groups and class organizations and brings up in bold relief the problems and contradictions as well as the options and other constraints available in a particular situation at a point of time. Constraint interaction between these forces leads to certain solutions and outcomes which may be intended or unintended, which may be more or less innovative. These, in turn, affect structures and processes which generate new problems and contradictions involving the actor as well as the options and the constraints available. The linkages between the various sets are so intricate that all of them affect and are affected through this entire process. Even the outcomes can in turn influence culture.

Action research aims to contribute to both practical concerns of people in an immediate problematic situation and the goals of social science by joint collaboration within a mutually acceptable ethical framework (Rapport, R. : 1970). The main difference between applied and action research lies in the fact that the former is not concerned to enlarge the stock of knowledge of the social science community but merely to use what exists. Action research is a type of applied social research different from varieties in the immediacy of the researcher's involvement in the action process. It is obvious that the intention of the parties is to be involved in change. Such change may involve the properties of the system itself. Thus action research puts a premium on direct involvement in organizational change. However, simultaneously it must provide increase in knowledge. There are two ways (Haller, F.A. : 1970) in which this can happen. First, when there is an attempt to test out and/or replicate theory in new setting by immediate involvement in the implementation phase of situation which constitutes a valid test of the theory. Second, by joining a situation in which a decision about action has been taken by members of the sponsoring system.

The role of the action sociologists is to document tne change process and provide feedback on the organizational change process so that it might be stopped, modified or accelerated. It is obvious that action research means involvement in developmental work rather than in routinized activities. It is distinguished by its special requirements in research methodology. The strategy for gaining the utilization of the research project has to be integrated with the research design at the start of the project itself. This requires the practitioner to devote considerable time to the creation of an infrastructure for receiving the findings and acting upon them. These considerations are central to carrying out activities which appear to be scientifically senseless but are designed to provide insight.

Action research has to be differentiated (Marris, P. and Rein, M : 1967) from summative evaluation. Action research purpose is tentative, non-committal and adaptive. It is focused on the next stage and evolves the future out of emergent opportunities. It has to interpret the present at the basis for inquiry. It attempts to comprehend a wide range of factors in a dynamic relationship. Summative evaluation, on the other hand, requires a clear and constant purpose. It proceeds with the logical development of steps and perceives the present situation in the context of the final outcome. It is not able to interpret the present until it knows answers to its ultimate questions. It focuses upon a limited range of factors.

There is an imperative need of action research in underdeveloped countries. Most of these countries are facing innumerable problems. There are numerous upheavals and the unrest of the people is expressed in various forms. People are torn between a number of ideologies each of which promises them emancipation from their bondages in the shortest possible time. Experience during the past 40 years has shown that there is lack of a sense of urgency and people are becoming impatient. In India, in particular, there are numerous research organizations both for natural and social sciences and they have all done good work but the results are seldom translated into action. It is, therefore, necessary that action research is carried out in various areas in accordance with the local requirements.

No scheme will provide the desired satisfaction unless we have clear objectives before us and seek participation of the people. We have to build on their knowledge, improve it wherever necessary and thereby stimulate action. Thus action research is a special type of research which is carried out by launching field projects to find out the workable solutions of the existing problems. It occupies an important place in socio-economic development of the country. Without its proper utilization, the acceleration of progress is held up as expansion of development programmes cannot be carried on a large scale with confidence and certainty. The existing programme content may be enriched by adding some new items and applying new methods and techniques. In spite of the soundness of certain programmes people may not be interested in their acceptance due to faulty means of communication. Social engineering has to play an increasingly valuable role in testing the efficacy of successful projects over large areas. As values are also changing it would be wrong to ignore them as, in their absence, the impact of results cannot be correctly assessed. In action research, the researcher has to work with a sense of commitment. He cannot remain neutral in respect of the overall impact of a particular programme. The human factors involved in a project have seriously to be taken into account. Action research is, therefore, a dynamic process which is essential for the successful implementation of given solutions.

While carrying out action research, four different stages have been identified. The first is the baseline survey or the situation analysis. In this the existing social and economic background of the area has to be surveyed. This would include the general reaction of the people to the programme and the extent of their response, positive or negative. This would also include a complete inventory of valuable resources and technical knowhow. On the basis of this survey programme planning is done and the project is launched in the field after fulfilling necessary requirements. Information pertaining to social behaviour and attitudes of the people is essential as it helps in comparing the results to be obtained after the action research project has been in the field for a reasonable time.

The second stage is that of current appraisal to find out how the action research project is faring in the field and whether proper progress in their implementation is being maintained. It would also see whether people at large are accepting them and, if not, why? Do the extension techniques have the necessary impact on the propagation of new ideas ? If not, can the techniques be improved upon, whether the assumptions and hypotheses taken for trials have been tested? For this work, research workers from different disciplines have to work as a team with proper coordination.

The third stage is where knowledge improvements and

modifications are sought to be introduced in the field as a result of concurrent evaluation. The overall impact of the programme is examined after these new interventions have borne fruit.

The fourth and final stage is that of the summative evaluation. The total outcome has to be studied to find out as to how traditional beliefs and practices have been affected and the extent to which the aims and objectives of the programmes have been achieved. Strong and weak points in this project have to be ascertained and documented. On the basis of these, practical recommendations can be made for the diffusion of the results of successful projects.

The research strategy for the action project is fourfold:

(a) *Survey of the availability of the technical knowledge and allied factors* — Under action research particular problems are identified and full details of its technical knowhow, its working efficiency, work done on it by various organizations or individuals, views of the people with regard to costs, economics of operations, social import, etc., should be found out in order to ascertain the correct position. In action research survey the combined expertise from various disciplines such as technology, social sciences, extension, etc., is to be used.

(b) *Study of attitudes* — It is necessary to find out the people's attitudes to the programmes. Efforts have to be made to counter the negative attitudes.

(c) *Study of records and documents* — Records available in Government resorts, municipal offices and other organisations have to be made use of. Sometimes examination of personal documents might also become necessary. Reports and case studies provide some authentic information. Statistics if available have an important bearing on a research.

(d) *Observation* — Observation is an important tool for action research. Observations may be made of individuals or of groups in specific areas of locality. The study of local culture helps in getting correct information on many socio-economic problems. This may sometimes be supplemented by interviews or case studies which will provide quantitative and qualitative aspects of the situation.

Sociology-based action research in India is a rare phenomenon. The

Planning Research and Action Institute, Lucknow is the only official organization engaged in action research in this country. It has been able to give some sound programmes for large-scale extension within and outside the State of U.P. and in some cases to some developing countries. It has worked in close collaboration with national and international organizations. Action research projects have been taken up in the fields of rural industries, rural health, soil conservation, cooperation, youth work, panchayats and mass communication.[2] One of its earliest successes was the popularisation of latrines in rural homes. Development of sulphitation units for the manufacture of crystal sugar on a small scale and their popularization through people's organizations and individuals has been another popular project. Such units have been established throughout the country and also in parts of Pakistan. The Institute has provided a lead in setting up youth programmes. The work done in the field of production of audio-visual material has also attracted wide attention.

Two decades back when a number of institutions were set up for training of extension officers for rural development work, it was envisaged that some villages will be attached with each of them for development work. These were called "adopted villages". Full responsibility for development in these villages was to rest with the faculty of the training centre. This was probably the only occasion in which an attempt was made to practise some action sociology. For a variety of reasons, however, the adopted villages scheme did not yield the expected results. Probably the commitment expected from the faculty was not forthcoming in an adequate measure.

There is ample scope for action sociology in the field of voluntary action. Committed and concerned sociologists can work with some of voluntary organizations. They can participate in the action programmes, document people's response to the programmes, highlight successes and failures, suggest modifications or innovations in the programmes and thus gain an insight into the processes of change working in a particular area. The sociologists can actively participate in the dynamic process of action, contemplation and action, which is the essence of praxis.

NOTES

1. Several action research projects have been undertaken. Prominent among them are listed below:

Swedish Action Research Project on Narcotic Addicts. Alam Touraine has reported on three action research projects involving movements of students, women and ecologists. Ake Sandberg has worked on the study of working life in Stockholm.

2. See *Action Research and its Importance in an Underdeveloped Economy.* Planning Research and Action Institute, Lucknow, 1963.

REFERENCES

Haller, F.A., "Group Feedback Analysis as a Change Agent", *Human Relations*, 23: 4, 1970.

Himmelstrand, U., *Innovative Processes in Social Change: Theory, Method and Social Practice* in Tom Bottomore, Stefan Nowak and Magdalene Sokolovoski, Sage Publications, London, 1982.

Lewin, K., *Resolving Social Conflicts,* Harper and Brothers, New York, 1948.

Marris, P. and Rein, M., *Dilemmas of Social Reform,* Atherton, New York, 1967.

Rapport, R.N., *Three Dilemmas in Social Research,* Social Science Research Council Conference, England, 1970.

2

ACTION SOCIOLOGY AND RURAL DEVELOPMENT

N.C. CHOUDHURY

During the past 30 years of my career as a social anthropologist I have been hearing, from time to time, a call from my professional colleagues to get involved in the problem of development so as to give a positive direction to the forces of change. One such recent call has come from no less a person than Prof. M.N. Srinivas. A few months ago while delivering the inaugural address on the occasion of the silver jubilee of the Southern Regional Offices of the Anthropological Survey of India, he asked the Sociologists and social anthropologists to actively participate in the development processes and tackle vital social problems. He also urged for the creation of a special cadre for social scientists in the lines of IAS, IPS and IFS from among sociologists with higher research qualifications.

The question that obviously comes to our mind is that even after the spectacular increase in the teaching and study of sociology during the past four decades why we have not been able to influence the policy-makers and planners so as to associate ourselves with social development. But at the same time it must be mentioned that sociologists during this period have made excellent studies on social problems like juvenile delinquency, crime, prostitution, drug addiction, problems of backward communities, tribal studies and a host of similar problems. We rarely come across studies in which a sociologist has directly participated in the planning and execution of a scheme for social development. In this Paper I will try to explore the causes of the gap between theory and practice and discuss the scope of the application of knowledge of sociology in tackling social problems with some concrete case studies.

Sociology makes a distinction between growth and development.

Growth generally means increase in the volume of goods and services but development implies a qualitative change in the capacities of a society to organize its activities more effectively. It implies structural changes in the form of relationship, development of new objectives, ideas and methods (Belshaw: 1977). We often talk about development with social justice, which means that the courses and forms of development should benefit the socially and economically backward more than the others. It is here, I believe, we can play some effective role.

The application of sociological knowledge to the problems of development has been done possibly in three ways: first, the diagnostic studies which are mainly concerned with finding the causes of backwardness, economic or socio-cultural, of a community. During the past two decades a large number of studies on tribal problems have been done by anthropologists and sociologists. These are mostly diagnostic type of studies; second, which may be called the prescriptive studies, the concern has been to prescribe specific course of action for solving some of the problems at hand. But such prescriptive studies are relatively few; third, in this fall the evaluatory studies, which are mainly to evaluate in concrete economic and social terms the benefits accrued from development programme.

We need not consider these categories as mutually exclusive. A prescription for a social problem, for instance, cannot be given without knowing the nature of the problem. Similarly evaluation of the benefits derived from a programme can be done better if the sociologists have a full grasp of the problem itself. In all the above type of studies the sociologist, besides understanding development from economic and technological points of view, stresses upon placing the problem of development in a cultural context related with the values and choice of the people. This human factor in development cannot be ignored, on it depends the success or failure of a programme.

Action sociology is directly concerned with the involvement of sociologists in all stages of development. This needs not only to find out the roots of the social problem and suggest its remedy but to associate ourselves with the diagnosis of the problem, planning, execution, monitoring and evaluation of the programme designed to solve the problem.

I do not know to what extent we, the sociologists, are prepared to meet this requirement. I feel that a big gap exists between what we teach and research and what is expected of us. If we wish to analyse the causes of his inadequacy, a sort of introspection, several factors come out very clearly. These are:

(1) The teaching and research of sociology in our Universities have more a theoretical and descriptive bias than developing specific tools and mechanism to apply to the solving of social problems. As a result we hardly know the conditions under which speedy development can take place with minimum counter-effect so as to lay the foundation for a lasting path to development.

(2) In devising a plan for social development it is often necessary to call upon the knowledge and expertise of a large number of specialists from other disciplines, namely, engineering, chemistry, medicine, agronomy, psychiatry, hydrology and a host of other subjects besides sociology. Sociology alone cannot cope with all the dimensions of a programme for development. With the rapid growth of science and technology it is becoming all the more imperative to use this knowledge in planning and execution of a programme. Sociologists who participate in a programme for social development must be able to communicate with other experts in this joint endeavour, which we are not at present mentally prepared to do. This means that sociologists should be able to understand what other experts are talking about and the extent to which their ideas and methods can be fitted into a particular programme.

(3) It is often found that plans and programmes for development are imposed from the top, in the preparation of which sociologists are rarely consulted. During the past three decades of planning we have not been in a position to break this impasse, may be because we have not voiced our objection strongly enough and also we have implicitly relied upon the administrators for the deliverance of the goods. The failure of this approach to planning is too well known to us to warrant a detailed discussion. But now that the strategy of planning has substantially changed from general to specific giving more attention to the local and felt needs of the people, the sociologists can play an effective role in the preparation and execution of such local plans.

I shall now dwell upon a few areas of rural development in which sociologists along with other experts can play an effective role.

(1) Problem of the rural poor—this is a complex social problem whose magnitude varies from area to area. In general it involves the problems relating to employment (partial or inadequate), low income, landlessness, educational and health problems. The Government of India has instituted the IRDP and other programmes in the plan period of 1980-85. A proper evaluation of these programmes at the block level is imperative to find out the shortcomings of the programmes in operation and suggest ways and means to overcome them. In general it has been observed that in the developing countries the status and condition of small farmers and peasants are rapidly declining from owner-farmer to part-owner, part-tenant, share-cropper and eventually to labourer. At the same time the income of farmers with access to new technology, inputs and services is increasing, resulting in a rapid widening of the gap in the rural areas between the rich and poor (Clark: 1989).

In this situation the sociologists can play a very important role.

Jain has suggested four aspects to be integrated into IRD planning and practice. These are goal-level integration, planning-level integration, practice-level integration and monitoring-level integration (Jain: 1985):

(1) Problem of ecology in rural areas—this problem is assuming a serious magnitude with rampant destruction of forest and other natural resources, over-grazing, pollution in rivers and atmosphere, unplanned disposal of human and animal waste, etc. The Government has implemented several plans and programmes to tackle these problems with which our involvement is yet very marginal.

(2) Problems of social inequality—this is perhaps the most difficult of the social problems for it is weaved in the values and traditions of the people whose eradication cannot simply be done by social legislation. Economic upliftment, alternative occupation may help to mitigate the problem to some extent but total eradication requires a sustained effort. I think sociologists can be more effective in devising plans to remove, or at least, minimize this form of inequality.

(3) Problem of backward classes, tribals and minorities—the problems concerning these people range widely from economic

to social, education, health and nutrition. Sometimes ethnocentric bias may hold up the cause of development. Action programmes relating to these people's development may be better understood by sociologists and anthropologists and, therefore, it is presumed that they can play a vital role in the planning and execution of programmes of their development.

I have just mentioned a few problem areas of rural development which need our immediate attention. There are many more aspects to these problems which need our attention equally well.

I shall now discuss two development programmes with which I and my colleagues were directly associated. The purpose is to show the nature or expertise we could render to these programmes.

(1) **Evaluation of ITDP in Jalpaiguri**

On the request from the Government of West Bengal we made an evaluation of the performance of ITDP in the Jalpaiguri district of West Bengal in 1984. The ITDP came into operation in this district in 1979. The ITDP consisted of a large number of schemes which could be classified into agricultural schemes, animal husbandry and livestock schemes and other schemes. Some schemes were meant for the community (drinking water, roads, adult education, minor irrigation schemes) and others improving the economic condition of individual persons. These included agricultural aid, animal husbandry, fish cultivation, village industries etc. An intensive study of beneficiaries in 13 villages situated in 4 out of 13 blocks in the district revealed that the programme had been unable to achieve its desired object.

We could identify several factors which have collectively brought about this state of affairs. Some of these factors are local and specific while others are more general which could hold true for ITDPs elsewhere:

(a) It was observed that proper assessment of the needs of the people was not made prior to the preparation and execution of the plan. For instance those wanting bullocks were given cows or pigs, those wanting agricultural loan had been given live-stock and so on. Only 35 out of 300 beneficiaries surveyed got what they wanted.

(b) The inputs available for distribution among the beneficiaries were often found inadequate or improper. For instance a block was given more pigs or goats whereas the demand was for bullocks. Naturally this led to improper use of inputs.

(c) The performance of public sector banks in disbursing loans to beneficiaries was not at all satisfactory. The bank did not consider all the beneficiaries, even though recommended by the local bodies, as creditworthy. This creates a contradiction between the stated goal of the project and mode of operation of the loan-giving institutions.

(d) Lack of co-ordination among various government agencies and programmes operating in an area often caused delay and improper implementation of a scheme.

(e) Somehow the schemes, particularly the community schemes, could not generate sufficient interest among the villagers to draw their participation at the desired level.

Even the elected village bodies have tended to become too institutionalized and bureaucratized and did not care to respond to the needs of the people (Choudhury and Bhowmick: 1986).

I have given above only the gist of our findings. A fuller report with recommendations was duly submitted to the Government with the hope that some of the observations would be taken note of to make necessary alterations in the administration of the schemes.

(2) **Impact of Irrigation Schemes in the Terai Region**

This study was also undertaken by me and my colleagues (Choudhury *et al.*: 1986) at the instance of the Government of West Bengal. The main objective of the study was to prepare a status report of the existing irrigation facilities in the Terai region with a view to identifying the schemes which have been partially or wholly successful in some blocks and to ascertain the reasons for their success. Another important aspect of the study was to find out the impact of the irrigation schemes upon the beneficiaries in terms of increase in crop production and income. A team of investigators under our guidance visited 30 villages (randomly chosen) and interviewed about 550 beneficiaries with a pre-coded questionnaire.

The data were processed through computer. In the preliminary report that we have submitted to the Government we have made a summary of 30 findings and discussed their implications in irrigation programmes for rural development. It will be unnecessary to discuss all these findings here but I will mention only a salient few:

(a) The irrigation schemes have benefited the small and marginal farmers (75%) more than the big and medium farmers.
(b) There is a wide variation in the adoption of a particular scheme in different regions and classes. For instance, STW has helped relatively more small, medium and big farmers than marginal farmers. In Cooch Behar dug-well is more common among medium and big farmers than among small and marginal farmers.
(c) In the entire Terai region 72 per cent of the beneficiaries have benefited from Government schemes and the rest from private resources. This shows the need to promote schemes to increase the number of private beneficiaries.
(d) In general the command area of a scheme is much less than what it should have been.
(e) Underutilisation of irrigation is determined by a number of factors: location of the plot, open-field channels, disputes over construction, right of way problem, poor maintenance, defective pipeline, silting, leakage, etc.
(f) The average use of irrigation from different sources is extremely low during the Kharif season. The demand for irrigation is highest in the Rabi season.
(g) The major causes of keeping land fallow both during pre-Kharif and Rabi seasons are percolation problem, unavailability of complementary inputs and lack of credit and capital.
(h) A major section of beneficiaries said that they had no control or say over the irrigation system. The participation rate is very low. This has often led to corruption, disputes and strained interpersonal relations.
(i) Inter-departmental co-operation in implementing and operating the schemes is rather poor. This has often led to delay and frustration among the people.
(j) Irrigation alone is not sufficient to intensify agriculture; getting the complementary inputs in time was also stressed upon by the beneficiaries.
(k) Irrigation has helped to marginally increased employment as labourer during the Rabi season but it has not been able to increase any female employment.

The above two examples are instances of evaluation studies of specific plans and programmes of development with an action orientation. The project is still continuing and it is expected that our findings would be utilized to make necessary modifications both at the planning level and at the execution level.

Social Welfare, Voluntary Agencies and Action Sociology

A large number of voluntary agencies, big and small, are engaged in social welfare activities for a very long time. Their activities have helped the Government in its efforts since 1956 to bring about planned social change. There is a basic difference between the approaches of these two agencies. The Government's plans and programmes are often well chalked out, multi-dimensional and cover large sections of population, often an entire State or a country. The scope of activities of the voluntary agencies, on the other hand, is limited to cover smaller populations with one or two programmes at a time. But the scope of utilizing the sociological knowledge at all the levels — planning, implementation and monitoring—is far greater here. In the case of government plans and programmes the bureaucratic constraints and the fact that they are often imposed from above give little flexibility to involve sociologists at the planning or execution level. But a voluntary agency working in the field of social welfare has the flexibility to modify its plans and programmes at any level of operation. I think Action Sociology has a good operational base in the work of these agencies.

An immediate example of this sort of application of sociological knowledge to welfare activities of a voluntary organization is the excellent work done by the Sulabh International in uplifting the socio-economic conditions of *Bhangis* and other backward classes. The work has possibly started as a social welfare programme with a definite objective in view and later on culminated into a multi-point programme. Here the success has been possible because of able leadership, proper input of technology, correct assessment of the needs of people and flexibility of the programme to modify itself according to the local conditions. I think it is a lesson for those of us who wish to see sociology used more and more in planning and development.

I would like to conclude this paper by saying that the State is more and more assuming the role of the principal social welfare agency. Crores of rupees have been spent on a large number of programmes but has the result been near to our expectation? We, as sociologists, have some social responsibility to minimize the rate of failure as far as possible. And for this we will have to modify the curricular of teaching of sociology and anthropology in our colleges and universities, develop proper tools and techniques for action sociology and, above all, divert our research and participatory interests to problems of relevant social issues. Perhaps through a process of trial and error we will be able to contribute our share in the development processes.

NOTE

1. *Decan Herald* dated 16-5-1986.

REFERENCES

Beleshaw Cyril, S., *Anthropology in the Development Process* ed by H.M. Mathur, New Delhi, 1977.

Bhowmick, S.K. and Choudhury, M.C., *Planning for Tribal Development: An Evaluation and Comments*, Calcutta, May, 1986.

Clark C. Camiron, *ASARRD and Small Farmers Development in Asia Bangkok* quoted from H.M. Mathur's article, "Reaching the poor in rural areas: Developmental issues and administrative requirement" in *Man and Development*, September, 1984.

Choudhury N.C., Mukhopadhyay R.S. and Subba T.B., *Survey on Impact of Existing Irrigation Schemes in Terai Region*, 1984 (mimeographed).

Jain, S.C., *Integrated Rural Development Programmes and Social Inputs in Rural Poor: Their Hopes and Aspirations* ed by Madhu S. Mishra, 1985.

3

ACTION SOCIOLOGY :
Some Reflections

JOSE KANANAIKIL

Speaking of Action sociology, I am reminded of a story concerning philosophers. A group of eminent philosophers were holding a serious discussion. The subject-matter of the discussion was about the number of teeth in the mouth of a horse. After heated discussions, the eminent philosophers could not come to any conclusion. Finally a young philosopher stood up and suggested that they go and look into the mouth of a horse. The whole assembly felt insulted at this most unbecoming suggestion from an inexperienced student of philosophy. The suggestion amounted to asking to give up the hallowed practice of deductive reasoning and taking recourse to observations of empirical data.

The reference to such a story in a meeting of sociologists may sound preposterous. However, I would submit that sociologists too are often inclined to build ivory towers for themselves instead of mingling with the life and reality of the common man which should be the basis for sociological theory and action.

For the past five years I have been engaged in an action research programme in Barh and Pandarak Blocks in Patna district. The following reflections are based on my experience of this programme.

When I started my programme five years ago, I began with visiting the Scheduled Caste *tolas* (hamlets) in the areas with a local companion. During these visits we tried to listen to what people had to say. Whenever we got a chance, we tried to share with them our conviction that no change would come about in their midst until they themselves came together and planned and worked together. In about six months we had a small following of about seven people. Together we started discussion how and what we could do to help the whole Scheduled Caste community in the area. We decided to form an organization which we called Bihar Dalit Vikas Samiti. Today we have nearly 10,000 members spread out in about 200 *tolas*, mainly in the two blocks. The organization is registered and self-training programme is going on.

We have a central office where we have about 40 full-time volunteers. They are paid a partial remuneration ranging from Rs. 200 to Rs. 500. The expenses of the association are met by contributions from voluntary agencies, Government projects and local contributions, in that order. We hope to reverse the order.

The volunteers at the centres are divided into different departments — village contact, organization, legal aid, education, health and development. The ultimate aim is to build up a strong people's movement through an integrated developmental approach. Each department tries to respond to the respective needs of the people but in full Coordination with other departments. Coordination is achieved through daily inter-departmental consultation and weekly evaluation among themselves. Sometimes outside help is sought for a deeper social analysis.

In the area of development our activities so far have been to identify the problems and to systematically study them, inform and educate the people about the various government programmes and how to apply for them, and initiate concrete projects which are both income-generating and social-conditions improving. Since nearly all the people are agricultural labourers, it is difficult to initiate my programme without outside support.

In education we have made an ambitious commitment to bring about 100 per cent literacy among the Scheduled Caste people in the age group of 6 to 50 in the area. About 50 units are already functioning by our own initiative and we are getting very good response from the people. Our efforts to get Government assistance for adult education have so far not been very successful.

In the area of health we have started a programme for immunization for children of the age group of six months to seven years and primary health education. We hope to complete the immunization programme in two years. Primary health education would require more personnel, more time and more resources. We are looking around for help to start a crash programme to make the health-for-all dream a reality in these blocks.

Perhaps the most active department in our organization is the legal aid cell. It consists of both legal education and legal aid. We conduct periodic camps for village leaders in legal education. We get an average of two to three cases a day. At present we manage to settle out of court more than 50 per cent of the cases that come to us.

One of the latest developments in our programme has been the training programme for the youth. This is a two-month programme during which the trainees are fully exposed to our work and methodology, to the village conditions and the functioning of the government administration. Weekly evaluation, personal diaries and reports and a three-day input at the beginning at the end are some of the features of our training programme. We take only 15 trainees at a time. Most of those who join us are college youth. We have already completed three such training programmes. We have at present a waiting list of more than 50 applicants. Lack of space and lack of resources have forced us to limit the number of trainees. The tremendous changes that come about in the young men within the short period of two months and the confidence they acquire is a matter of great satisfaction.

From my experience, I have selected three areas that have important consequences for sociological thinking and, therefore, for action sociology.

Does societal change come about through planning from above or through action from below? Without going into a discussion on the filter down theory the consensus theory or the conflict theory. I will simply state here that our field experience has convinced us that no meaningful social change can ever take place unless there is concerted action, a social movement, from below. Planning policy decisions and welfare programmes from above can definitely support a social movement but they cannot replace it. Action from above here also refers to the role of voluntary organizations and of research scholars who often tend to work *for* the people but often not *with* the people.

Action from below has three ingredients: motivation, organization and resources for action. It is only when people in villages and towns become convinced about the need for change, become sufficiently organized for action, and have the means at their disposal to launch out action programmes that they can make a difference in society. Everything else is a means to assist in this process. Hence the question is not one of "either/or" but one of combining in the right proportion. How do we engage in planning from above and at the same time identify ourselves with the aspirations and the felt needs of the people? In other words, how do we transform administrative policies and sociological theories into the dynamics of a social movement?

The lack of proper integration between policy decisions and people's aspirations have serious consequences. One of them is the introduction of programmes which are not really beneficial to the people at all or for which they are not ready. Another consequence is that serious research findings are not taken into consideration or are not even encouraged. A third consequence is that since most of the decisions are made by administrators, they necessarily become a part of government machinery and often an instrument of party policies. Often such programmes end up as purely economic programmes on paper. They are neither properly implemented nor are the various social and cultural dimensions taken into account. While so much is talked about evils of communalism, for example, it is sad to note that it is often the same people who preach the evils of communalism that often engage in fanning the communal virus for their own self-interest.

Although we have the Integrated Rural Development Programmes (IRDP), there is very little integration in most of the programmes initiated by the Government. For too long have we mixed up development process with administrative procedures. An administrator friend of mine told me some time ago when I shared with him this concern, that it would be practically impossible to have an integrated approach. No department can be expected, he said, to have a comprehensive understanding of any problem nor is it sufficiently equipped to implement any integrated development programme which takes into account various aspects related to other departments. Our administrators, brought up on the British tradition of law and order approach, are not only not equipped to deal with developmental aspects in all their complexity, but also they are often overworked with administrative aspects and have little time left to engage in serious developmental activities.

Lack of integration leads to compartmentalization and red-tapism. Often what one department plans or does is not known to other. An individual looking for information in related areas will be asked to go to different people in different departments. Often he will be sent from one place to another without receiving the information he is looking for. This leads to corruption and red-tapism.

Much has been written on the uniqueness of caste in Indian Society, and the relationship between caste and class. Definitely, caste can be seen as a form of social stratification just as atrocities can be looked at as a form of power relationship in society. But a closer look at the Indian Society forces us to recognize the fact that both social stratification and frequent atrocities against the Scheduled Castes have deeper roots in the ethnically rooted caste identities as forms of social organization, social competition and social control. Both the instinct for self-preservation and the fear of others make groups to cling to their caste-based group to control power; they use it to strengthen the hold of their own caste in society. Sociologists and administrators have not given sufficient attention to this reality when they make social analyses, develop social policies or when they are engaged in search for alternatives.

I would like to give a concrete example to show how all this affects the life of the people especially in the rural areas. Before I came here for this meeting, I went to visit our field unit. More than 50 per cent of the people there were suffering from inflammation of the eyes — conjunctivitis — or were just cured of it. Is anyone concerned about it? But all of us have often been informed on TV about the danger of AIDs. Whose needs and whose fears get priority?

When the Asian Games were being inaugurated at the Jawaharlal Nehru Stadium, I felt proud that India could possess such a beautiful stadium which could seat 75,000 people. Today I also like to watch colour TV or to hear about what the super-computers can do. But it also makes me feel sad and all this is happening in a country where nearly half the people go to sleep hungry and where millions of people in the rural areas live without safe drinking water. A study we conducted in two *panchayats* showed that out of 15 hand-pumps installed by the Government 13 were out of order in less then six months. It was not because people did not care for them. The hand-pump pipes had not been put deep enough in the first place. No strainers had been put on them and the nuts and bolts had not been fixed properly. These were all Scheduled Caste *tolas*.

The area where I work is prone to floods every year. When the place is flooded, the only means of communication for people is boats. A few boats which ply around belong to or are used by the upper castes. Even when the area is not flooded, there are no connecting roads for most of the villages. People have to walk 3-5 km or more to reach the nearest road.

If the physical conditions are bad, the social conditions are worse. Nowhere in the world do people have to pay interest more than 20-25 per cent a year. But the poorest people in the world — the Scheduled Castes and Scheduled Tribes in India — are paying from 8 to 10 per cent or more interest every month in the rural areas. The area where I work, barely 50 km from Patna, people are being paid three rupees or an equivalent as daily wages!

The problem of living space is a night-mare for most Scheduled Caste people in the rural areas. The little space where 10 or 15 families huddled together 10 to 16 years ago have today double the population but they live in the same space with absolutely no space to expand.

Perhaps most pitiable situation is the functioning of the legal system. It is a common practice among the upper castes in the rural areas to implicate the people of the Schedule Castes in fabricated cases whenever they do not like someone or want to "teach a lesson" to some Scheduled Caste person. All that they have to do is to inform the police, and police take care of the rest. The poor man will be involved in court case which drags on for the next six to eight years — years of harassment and often starvation. Every time he goes to the court he loses his day's work. He has to pay to the lawyer and to the court clerk. The case may hang on indefinitely. Who cares?

I would like here to present some concrete suggestions for follow up. An Action Sociologist, I understand, is one who is convinced that, in order to be an authentic sociologist, he has to transform his convictions into action both in his individual life and in the society to which he belongs. He must derive his concepts, theories and ideology from the life experience of the people. He definitely tries to profit from the existing concepts, theories and ideologies which exist in the field of sociology but, in the ultimate analysis, his convictions and commitments are shaped by these experiences of the people. Hence, being an Action Sociologist today is neither a luxury nor a fad but a sacred duty of all sociologists to be true to themselves, to translate their convictions into action, to practise what they preached. It is a call to go and look into the mouth of the horse instead of having a theoretical discussion on the number of teeth in a horse's mouth.

One meets at least two types of sociologists today. First, there are those who get a degree in Sociology and are engaged in writing and/or teaching in some colleges or universities. How to translate their ideas into action is not often their primary concern. Then there are those who may or may not have a degree but are engaged in some social action. Many of these may also be committed to one or the other ideology.

Often they are so involved in the action programmes that they have no time to reflect on what is going on, or to critically review their assumptions and theories. Today we need sociologists who remain rooted in the life experiences of the people, who have the courage to respond to the various social problems facing the country and, at the same time, can subject themselves to serious intellectual discipline in order to classify their assumptions and to build new models and to find new answers.

What an individual can achieve by himself or herself is often very limited. This holds good also for action sociologists. To be effective, it is important for them to come together, to share experiences and to be mutually supported by one another. It is a matter of great satisfaction for all involved in action sociology that this Seminar has resolved to establish an Indian Association for Action Sociology. Such an association would be greatly beneficial to build linkages among action sociologists, to articulate the meaning of social action that is already taking place in different forms and in different parts of the country, and to give direction and guidance to new ventures. It will also be able to influence universities to remodel existing sociology courses to make them more action oriented and to introduce newcomers to prepare the students to respond to the needs of the time both through action programmes and through serious search for conceptual and theoretical classifications.

4

THE NEED FOR ACTION SOCIOLOGY

A.K. LAL

During its brief existence in India sociology "has tried to answer questions relevant to the discipline, though in the particular context of the Indian society" (Mukherjee: 1976). It has been concerned with the practical affairs of the society also. Sociological findings and perspectives have been useful in examining social issues. Attempts have been made to establish a link between scientific knowledge and concrete social problems. The findings of the sociological studies have been helpful in drafting the programmes of social change. Sociologists in some cases have helped the Government in framing the policy of development as scientists and advisers. A few so-called "critical researches" are reported to have "exposed perfidies and untruths" suggesting alternatives for a better future (Das: 1983).

In spite of all these, the sociological studies have not been put to systematic use for effective and sustained development. Sociologist's contributions to the solutions of the society have not been that marked. Their efforts at most amount to scratching the surface. Social comments without any responsibility for sociology amounts to "standing on the sideline and carp"! A great deal of research turns out to be the pursuit of triviality. There is considerable unease in taking up major issues for investigation. The most astonishing fact is the assumption by sociology of the role of a master and not a servant. Instead of becoming a means it has turned out to be an end. Sociologists have remained "expert witness" to the process of change. Intervention for change has not attracted their attention. Self-imposed isularity seems to have led them to the brink of self-destruction. Research and consultancy alone cannot usher much impact. These lead people to question "the working tradition" in social sciences in general and sociology in particular. The very logic behind supporting this expensive symbol of futility and its related infrastructure is being challenged now (Mathur and Sethi: 1983).

Today sociology is in a stage where its radical reorientation for the welfare of the society is needed. Sociologists have to provide valuable help in solving delicate, and potentially explosive problems of the society. It can no longer afford to remain an academic luxury. sociologists have to be actively responsive to the challenges of the society. They have to be action-oriented. Intervention for change has to be the primary responsibility of action sociologist. There is no substitute for action-oriented endeavours. Understanding of the situation and doing something about that have to be the primary concern of sociologists. Society should be the immediate recipient of the benefits of the scholarship of sociologists. They have to be the catalysts completely involved in the process of change. Doing something about the people is the real challenge that sociologists have to confront. Action sociology, however, should not be viewed merely as a recent addition to the evergrowing pluralism characterizing the discipline of sociology. It is in fact poised to emerge as a major contemporary influence to take up the issues afflicting the society. It will help bridge the long neglected gap between the theoretical concerns of sociology and the interests of society. Action sociologists are like Redfield's "fellowmen . . . assuming new difficulties and new responsibilities". They have to shoulder unprecedented responsibilities.

II

The success of the Sulabh in its different programmes for the welfare of society reminds sociologists of their potentialities in solving the long neglected problems. The fact that social intervention by action sociologists is capable of producing changes of unprecedented magnitude finds strong corroboration in the experiences of the Sulabh strategies for change. This is a strategy representing a positive programme of action. It has combined the process of helping and learning through social action. The intervention through Sulabh represents deliberate and conscious effort to induce systematic change so that people get appropriate sanitation facilities leading to the uplift of those that occupy the base of the traditional hierarchical system. The Sulabh technology of excreta disposal is a small-scale enterprise which is cheap, locally manageable, efficient and fulfils the conditions for being called modern and scientific. It puts a heavy premium on smallness and self-sufficiency. It is small-scale and resource-efficient. In fact its simplicity and smallness makes it appropriate to meet the local need. It is a technology that is "appropriate" to the particular situation faced by the people of the developing nations. The technology is appropriate on economic and factor endowment grounds. Its relevance transgresses the boundaries of states and regions. In fact the interest that it has evinced is transnational in character. Capital intensive technology and financial bottlenecks have virtually created a situation of stagnation and under-development. The Sulabh technology of excreta disposal, therefore, represents a choice between modern growth and traditional stagnation. In order to ensure pragmatism the developing countries are required to scale down their expectations of solving the sanitary problems of the underdeveloped through the technology suited for the developed. Borrowed concepts and imparted methodology can hardly be a substitute for appropriate technology so long as they are not attained to the existing realities. The Sulabh endeavours at the same time do not represent the echoes of an already outdated counter culture movement. It is appropriate no doubt but at the same time it does not represent a hangover from our feudal past. It is not a throwback to an earlier tradition. In fact it is qualitatively different from the forms that have been rendered obsolete. In the most significant way it reflects a typical response to the interventional activities of an institution committed to action sociology.

It also represents an investment in man as it provides amelioration of the downtrodden. The emerging cultural norms of our social system favour its spread. It is not a scheme having commercial intentions. A lot of social planning is involved. It would not be an exaggeration to maintain that the choice of this technology is linked with the emerging values of Indian social system. In fact social values seem to have played a substantial role in the selection of the technology.

The change that is being witnessed in the field of sanitation and upliftment of the downtrodden has not been forced from above. An action sociologist provides alternatives leaving the target group the right to self-determination. The people of course, are made aware of the innovation being introduced. The ultimate initiative for the adoption comes from within. Through its concerted efforts the Sulabh is not using sociology in a fairly wider context. It is an instance of development made by the people with the active intervention of the practitioners of the social science.

III

The above discussion should not lead to the conclusion that sanitation and uplift of the scavengers is the only suggested area where sociology can be put to use. In fact many more problems are there. One has to locate them to analyse them in depth and their ramifications for the purpose of fixing strategies for intervention. Poverty and ignorance are important factors afflicting our society. Programmes for intervention cannot afford to put a gloss over them. People's participation in development should similarly constitute an important item of the agenda of the action sociologist. Problems of the weaker sections and rural development should also be accorded upper priority. Local initiatives to ensure self-sufficiency in the economy and programmes of self-employment for the youth have to be activated with vigour. Elimination of socio-psychological barriers inhibiting change and keeping people perpetually in deep slumber of inaction and passivity also deserve the attention of the action sociologist. This list is simply illustrative and not exhaustive. Action programmes however, have to be drawn up in the manner that would ensure effective management of social change. The need is to initiate processes to first solve those problems that require immediate attention. Pending ultimate cure tentative remedies would also do.

To be an effective interventionist, sociologist's familiarity with the basic conceptual frameworks of the discipline as well as methods of collection of social facts and their analysis is a basic necessity. In fact "knowledge should precede and undergrid whatever techniques are used to solve practical problems" (Morland: 1966).

In any programme action sociologists have to put a heavy reliance on intensive fieldwork. Objective appraisal of the situation is needed more in a society, where each stage of development is transient to some new stage. Sol Tax's (1950) hesitation in accepting "action anthropology except in the contest of fieldwork to acquire knowledge about the circumstances and existence to change" is equally valued in the case of action sociology. The facts and processes unleashed in the wake of development through intervention have to be analysed to obtain sound feedback. However so-called independent research designed and executed only in terms of the best principles of scientific methodology does not appear to be of much applicability to action sociologists.

REFERENCES

Das, A.N., "The Role of Social Scientists in Action Research" *in Action Research for Development* (Ed) by Kuldeep Mathur and Harsh Sethi, Indian Institute of Public Administration, New Delhi, 1983.

Mathur, K. and Sethi, H., "Introduction" to Action Research for Development. Indian Institute of Public Administration, New Delhi, 1983.

Morland, J.K., "Race Relations Activities of Sociologists" in *Sociology in Action* (Ed) by Aurhu B. Shostak, Dorsey Press, Illinois, 1966.

Mukherjee, R.K., "Indian Sociology: Historical Development and Present Problems" *in Social Sciences and Social Realities* (Ed) by S.C. Dube, Indian Institute of Advanced Study, Simla, 1976.

Sol Tax "Action Anthropology" in *Anthropology and Tribal Welfare in India* (Ed) by L.P. Vidyarthi, Ranchi, 1959.

5

NATURE, SCOPE AND SUGGESTED CONTENTS OF THE POSTGRADUATE COURSE ON ACTION SOCIOLOGY

A.D. SINGH

An attempt has been made in this paper to present before you some raw materials for the proposal to include a special paper on Action Sociology at the post-graduate level. Those who are academically conservative may feel that what is proposed here falls more in the arena of other branches of learning and there is not much of Sociology. This is certainly correct if we remain rigid about the nature and scope of sociology as it is accepted today. In fact a rethinking at the fundamental level about the role of sociologists in society is really necessary.

Whereas in the field of professional learning like medicine, engineering, accountancy, etc., there is a provision towards the end of the course to arrange for the practical training of the students, there is hardly any such provision for those who are trained as social scientists including sociology. Of course psychology has branched itself off into various areas like education, industry, etc., and with the help of laboratories has also arranged for imparting some skills which help psychologists to start certain vocational careers like psychiatry.

Sociologists have lagged behind and have not commonly used any social laboratory or social skills workshop to enable even the experts in this field to help solve any social problem. It is certainly not the idea to aim at making a sociologist Jack of all trades and master of none but it is also not satisfying to see an eminent sociologist looking at a bio-gas plant with wonder and feeling that this is a subject-matter for engineers only.

A sociologist must be able to face life, understand the same and also contribute to the solution of everyday problems. If he builds a home, he should not be totally dependent on engineers or if he rears some cattle and has some agricultural land he should be able to handle these problems and set up a bio-gas plant for his own use. If he is so equipped with the basics of social life, arts and artifacts he will prove himself a worthy citizen of his country.

An outline of a draft syllabus on "Action Sociology" has been, therefore, attempted for presentation before this galaxy of eminent sociologists. It is not a sacrosanct packet, you can tear it into pieces. But your effort must be constructive so that what you throw off should be suitably replaced. With this hope I venture to suggest the contents of the syllabus in "Action Sociology".

A Draft Syllabus for the Special Paper—Action Sociology

Paper IV—Nature and Scope of Action Sociology

1. What is Action Sociology? It means the use of sociological knowledge for the betterment of living standard, quality of life and all-round development of mankind.
2. Understanding life and its actual problems. Break-up of these problems into man's basic and other needs like food, clothing, shelter, water, energy, etc. The manner in which society organizes itself to fulfil these needs and the individual equips himself to avail himself of the same different economic, social and cultural settings.
3. Action Sociology prepares an individual to solve some of the basic problems which face him in everyday life by enabling him to acquire some skills pertaining to agriculture (for fulfilling the need for food), maintenance of devices for water supply (tube-wells, handpumps, etc.), spinning and weaving, house-building, cooking, low-cost sanitary devices, bio-gas, electricity, other sources of energy, etc.
4. Action Sociology should also cover the basic skills of family and social living like the procedures for getting enlisted as a voter, filing nominations, etc., organizing a cooperative, maintaining the minutes of the meeting, even running a meeting, First Aid, etc.
5. It should also include other skills which govern the economic, social, cultural and other aspects of an individual in society.
6. The exact scope of Action Sociology shall depend on the manner

in which society has organized itself for fulfilling its needs and wants. (Build-your-own-home concept in the USA). It has to co-exist with social life and human relationships.

7. It aims at equipping an individual with the minimum necessary scientific knowledge and technical skills to face the actual life situation in all circumstances. It helps individual to be more self-reliant and also of use to others.
8. Action sociology also covers sensitivity training which helps to change attitudes and prepares an individual to function in a group in a more harmonious and smoother manner.

Paper V—The Basic Skills of Social Living

1. Individual attitudes and values—acceptability, flexibility, etc., in terms of social conduct. How to conduct oneself in the present economic, social and cultural setting.
2. How to resolve conflicts in one's own home and in the social life—Honesty *vs* Corruption; Self *vs* the Rest, Communal, caste, religious, regional and such considerations *vs* Humanistic approach; Trade-off between money and power even social values; Social institutions like marriage *vs* Market mechanism; Clashes of ego, its consequences and remedies, etc.
3. The family welfare—its ingredients, how to build up a small happy family, the techniques of family planning.
4. How to become a family doctor and the limits of the same.
5. Case studies of some of the basic problems of family and social life.
6. How to make a house and a home? Different types of materials and their actual use.
7. How to get a well constructed and a handpump installed—their maintenance and working.
8. How to get best from the land—some farming knowledge, skills and techniques; fertilisers and their use; methods of cultivation and use of various tools and implements.
9. How to handle the spinning wheel (one *Amber Charkha* if run for one hour per day can make one person self-sufficient in clothing). How to weave, its basic technique, how to run a loom.
10. The basic skills of an electrician for setting right domestic and other common electrical problems.
11. How to construct various types of latrine and maintain them.

12. How to construct a bio-gas plant and maintain the same.

Paper VI—Understanding Society's (Official and Non-official) Techniques of Organizing Social Living for a Better Life

1. The official programmes in rural and urban areas for improving the standard of living and quality of life. What are these programmes? How to participate in and contribute to the same?
2. How to organize a literacy class and educational institutions. How to run the same?
3. How to form cooperative societies—their use and abuse. How to run the same?
4. Planting and rearing of trees of various types—their use and environmental necessity.
5. The basics of cooking. How to run a small hotel?
6. How to organize a shop—know the sources of supply and field of marketing, also the proper pricing principles.
7. Techniques of promoting national integration. How to get more persons involved in it?
8. Imparting skills which will help people towards self-employment—laundry techniques, hair-dressing and beauty treatment, watch repairing, radio and television repairing, leather goods manufacturing, motor repairing, motor driving, TV repairing, etc.

III

NEED FOR SOCIAL INTERVENTION

6

CONTINUITY WITHOUT CHANGE :
A Perspective Paper on Education

ALI ASHRAF

Some five years ago, a report of the New Education Policy was proposed by the Human Resource Development Ministry, Government of India, with great fanfare. This year the Government of India appointed a Committee to review the New Education Policy in order to suggest measures to remove the persistent and widespread illiteracy, elitism, unemployment and alienation in our education system, to give a work and employment orientation to education and to use it as an instrument of social reforms for a humane and enlightened society.

The Review Committee has published what it calls *A Perspective Paper on Education* and has circulated it for reactions and comments. It is a sad commentary on the educational system of the country that the problems of education have been mounting in spite of several educational commission reports prepared by very distinguished educationists. The state of education in India has been moving consistently and steadily towards distortions as well as degeneration. The problems are compounded as they cannot be confined to the field of education as it is bound up with all other spheres of national life. The Kothari Commission in 1966, acknowledging the contributions of earlier Commission, said that what we need is action.

We are, however, confronted with the problem not only of inaction but also of wrong action. The inaction by and large lay in the failure to take steps towards the achievement of universal literacy and reorienting the education system towards the needs of the people. The wrong action was evident in government policy in promoting vertical growth of an educational system that was basically ill-conceived and disoriented at the school level and has lacked the clear focus and unity of national goal at the level of higher learning. It seems that the overall degeneration in the educational system has taken place not merely for want of action but also for want of understanding. The attempts at reform of education have suffered from the defects of going along the colonial system of education without regard to changing needs and dynamic goals of independent India. The defects of the earlier system arose from the growing discrepancy between the erstwhile colonial educational system and its inability to solve our problems in the light of the objectives of a national policy and perspective. The problems, therefore, reflects a failure since Independence to identify the goals of freedom and to forge effective and adequate means of national regeneration. In many ways this failure reflected a reversal of the main objectives of the national movement and freedom struggle.

There is no doubt that the educational system has suffered for want of firm implementation of some of the national goals such as universal literacy. It is indeed a matter of profound regret that even after more than 43 years of Independence, we have not been able to achieve significant progress towards the goal of universal literacy. It is increasingly recognized that literacy, important as it is in itself, is also a key to other social improvements. The regions with high literacy have moved towards social development, health, maternity, and child welfare, more than other regions lagging behind in literacy, especially of the women. And yet we have been able to achieve no more than 36 per cent of literacy and our people comprise 50 per cent of the world's illiterate. Illiteracy indeed seems to be the curse of this sub-continent and the factor most responsible for its backwardness.

There are other problems in the field of education which are crying for reform. The government policy in the past, has however, followed the path of least resistance, and instead of tackling the problems where they exist, the Government followed the policy of shifting the ground, ditching the old institutions and founding the new ones in the name of specialization or excellence. For the past 30 years the universities and other educational institutions have been declining, and little has been done to arrest their decay. At the same time new institutions outside the traditional framework of universities were set up with massive financial support from the Central Government. This might have been a good idea if the new centre of excellence did not create a sense of complacency and a false sense of national progress towards new heights in the production of scientific and technical personnel.

II

The present Government shows a sensitivity towards the indigenous needs of our people and an awareness of the need to move the nation, in the words of the former Prime Minister, Mr. Vishwanath Pratap Singh, from independence to freedom. Independence from the colonial rule was necessary to make us masters of our destiny, but we did not use this opportunity to fashion tools of our national regeneration and freedom, in terms of capability to solve our problems and build the social infrastructure of a successful modern nation. The present Government is moving in the direction of some reorientation in its policies concerning education and employment, and hence the Review Committee has as its Chairman an eminent Sarvodaya leader with an acknowledged record of social service. The choice of such a Chairman as well as the statement of concerns expressed in the resolution constituting the Review Committee are indications of a new orientation on the part of the Government of India, and its present commitment to the reorganization of Indian society through new policies in the field of education, employment and rural development.

The Review Committee Paper shows serious concern over the persistent backlog of widespread illiteracy and the gross alienation and unemployment attending our educational system. There is also some concern over the influence of casteism, communalism and obscurantism in the educational institutions. And the purpose of the Perspective Paper is spelt out as the evolution of a framework which would enable the country to move forward towards an egalitarian and secular social order. Three objectives are specially mentioned which appear to be the guiding principles for the Review Committee. These three "basic concerns" of the government policy and the Review Committee, are: one, the Right to Work; two, the Unity and Integrity of the Nation; three, the Improvement of the Inner Man in India.

The Perspective Paper makes recommendations for many reforms in the educational system. This includes measures towards universal literacy and also to use the method of neighbourhood school or common school system as a step towards social equality. The common school system, suggested by the Kothari Commission in 1966, is a correction to the highly flaunted proposal for the establishment of a modern school in every district (Jawahar Navodaya Vidyalaya) which was rightly considered elitist, and was essentially escapist in that it isolated the model school from the problems of the other schools and the general environment of the country.

The Paper is right in its approach towards reform of the school education and in asserting that "the school should open up and non-formalize in creative ways" and rightly says that this would be better than building up an exclusive parallel system of non-formal education for the poor and working children. Creative non-formal education responding to the need patterns of dropouts or leftouts such as the working child, girls who cannot attend schools and children in unserved habitation or social situation can play a supportive and more importantly a challenging role in society during the transitional phase so that there is a continuous pressure on the school to open up and non-formalize itself. The Paper is also right in reiterating the use of mother tongue as the means of facilitating learning, self-expression and promotion of social identity of the child.

The Paper contains a number of ideas and measures towards the reform of higher education. But these ideas and reforms are mentioned in one breath without taking into account the earlier experiments with these reforms and their general failure to solve the problems and produce the desired results. It says, "the major innovative measures proposed for non-formalizing formal education, empowering people further, equalizing educational opportunities for women's education, modularization and semesterization of courses, replacement of the public examination systems by continuous, comprehensive, internal evaluation, decentralized management of education and linking university courses with development call for the teacher being placed at the centrestage". This is indeed quite a mouthful and each of the various measures calls for careful examination and not only from the point of view of their rationality but also from that of their feasibility under the circumstances of ground reality which are nothing short of a nightmare. These ideas of reforms are mentioned in one breadth without taking into account the earlier experiments and their general failure to bring about an improvement. There seems to be no realization that these reforms could not succeed in the congestion, purposelessness, indiscipline and irregularities prevailing in universities and colleges. It is not enough to recommend these reforms: it is necessary to examine the environmental conditions required for their success.

III

The objective of educational regeneration demands not only reform to improve and strengthen the present system but also to change and reorient the direction and purpose of education so as to serve as an instrument of nation-building and socio-economic development. The experiment with many of the earlier reforms foundered on the rock of corruption in the educational institutions and the mad rush for entry into professional courses or civil services. The discrete measures of reform could succeed only in an environment that was elitist and secure in the job prospects or free from the widespread pressures for admissions to courses of higher learning. The fact of the matter is that the system has virtually broken down in all institutions except a few central universities and institutes. The need, therefore, is to address to the problems of the educational system in the light of the social objectives of the nation. Moreover, a policy document such as the Perspective Paper cannot be content to document, true but trivial statements: instead it should stick its neck out to identify certain critical areas for a break-through in our educational system which is both inadequate and defective and essentially unrelated to the vital needs and goals to national development. If the vertical growth of the present educational system is allowed to continue, the magnitude of pressures on institutions of higher learning will increase and get out of control with the increase in literacy and population. As an inevitable result the number of unemployed educated youth will rise manifold and the nation will be faced with the colossal problem of coping with the half-baked graduates unfit for anything other than swelling the army of discontented and angry young agitators.

IV

An area of great significance is the vocationalization of secondary education. The idea was mooted decades ago as a measure to make the school education terminal for those who would receive training in some vocation and enter into employment or self-employment after the school education. This should be considered sufficient for majority of the students and would have the additional advantage of reducing the pressures on the institutions of higher learning. A common experience, however, is that vocationalization has proved a flop and socially useful productive work has proved to be more ritual.

This is a serious matter but the Perspective Paper does not examine the causes underlying the failure of vocationalization except reiterating its importance for all without any distinction. The failure of vocationalization reflects the persistence of the Macaulay paradigm, i.e. education as a means of gaining government employment. The students go to schools not to learn a vocation but on a fishing expedition in the hope of something to turn up and at best to pursue their education to enter the civil services, or lucrative professions. In fact the vocational training in our society is part of the family trade and business and children learn the traditional art and craft in their own families. The problem is that children either grow up following their caste/family occupations without going to school or go to a school of a kind that uproots them from their traditional occupations and renders them useless. An effective method and organization to combine occupational training with general education in order to raise the status of those employed in traditional arts and crafts is necessary. The issue is not of giving these children vocational training in schools but combining the family training with functional literacy in a school. This applies also to children who work for wages and still need to be given lessons in functional literacy. This is where non-formalization of school education is important and it may even require a subsidy from the Government to make up for the loss of training or income while the children attend their schools.

For the rest, it is not clear why technical training in maintenance and repair of machines, laboratories, vehicles, computers, radio and television and other daily gadgets of modern life cannot be devised. The demand for mechanics and overseers has been steadily increasing, and these are avenues for self-employment. Like literacy, this sector has been sadly neglected while elitist schools have taken long strides. The technical education of the bulk of our youth at the maintenance and repair level would go far in tackling the problem of employment and also of national productivity. Instead the country put higher priority on technical education of a higher order. The famous Indian Institutes of Technology are institutions of world class but 35 per cent of the scientists and engineers produced in India are known to migrate to other developed countries and many others seek jobs in civil services and management, and those who find jobs in industry are dissatisfied on account of mismatch between their training and the needs of the industry. There is a basic conflict between excellence and relevance.

This applies to medical education also where the Government under the advice and pressure of the Indian Council of Medical Education regarding higher standards in medical education has not been able to think out paramedical education and training on a large scale so as to produce enough paramedical staff to serve the needs of the masses of people. The engineers and doctors, like the urban elite in general, rarely find it attractive to work in the rural areas. It is important to consider whether or not the Government should consider more ITIs or Polytechnics and medical schools for training in technology or medicine which may not be of very high order but whose alumni may be more readily available to the masses of our people living in the slums and the villages. This is not to argue for unequal standards of facility but to emphasize that it would be better to provide the villagers with some services rather than to deprive them of services in the name of quality of excellence.

V

Beyond these reforms looms large the nature and purpose of education. Education is much more than a passport for employment; it is also formation of individual character. Moreover, education must also perform the function of training for citizenship. The educational system in India not only promotes elitism, it is also fraught with alienation. It lacks the socialization necessary to foster the values of citizenship, patriotism and the vision of a good and great society for the country. Education must provide the basis for a civic culture which binds all the people of the country into a common culture of civility. This is more than a matter of moral values or theological studies which as pursued in educational institutions are often ill-conceived and ineffective, and involves a moral underpinning of public life as well as personal life of the citizens.

It should be realized that when we harp on values such as democracy, secularism, socialism, etc., as the Perspective Paper does we only repeat the values handed out to us by the West and the past regimes and fail to spell out the specific implications of these values in the context of social objectives of the present times. It is, therefore, not enough to mention democracy but necessary to emphasize participation, decentralization and autonomy. Likewise, it is not enough to mention secularism but necessary to emphasize pluralism as well as equal respect for all religions. It is certainly not enough to mention socialism, for it is under review all over the world, but necessary to emphasize social solidarity, equality and justice for all, especially the traditionally downtrodden.

Above all, it is necessary to emphasize the values and virtues of citizenship without any occupational, social or ethnic distinctions. The nation needs a new culture, a new outlook on work and wages. The British departed but the legacy of bureaucratic superiority still lingers. The caste hierarchy reinforces the tendency of contempt towards the so-called "menial jobs". The carpenter or tailor does not command the social prestige that even a government peon commands. It is because of the wrong attitude towards social hierarchy and relatively low wages paid to those who perform so-called "lowly" jobs. A significant raise in wages for "lowly" occupations and a change in outlook showing dignity of labour and human equality must be a cardinal quality of the new education system.

The final point that calls for a comment is the management of education and educational institutions. The fact is that educational institutions have suffered because of extreme political interference and control not only by the Government but also by political persons and dominant groups who have used these institutions to further their social and political ends. It is important that educational institutions should be protected from unacademic tendencies and forces. This does not mean that the educational system should be cut off from society. It only means that the educational goals should be laid down by the popular and authoritative bodies, but once they are laid down their pursuit and implementation should be immune from political pressures and left to academics. It is also wrong to think that decentralization and autonomy in themselves will lead to the solution of the educational problems. In fact in educational institutions we need discipline as much as democracy. It is a curious phenomenon in our country that those who are entrusted with the responsibility of solving problems are precisely the ones who are responsible for the perpetuation of those problems. This unfortunately applies to the teachers also.

It would be a serious mistake to look upon education in isolation from the other sectors of social life. We are witnessing today a tremendous urge towards upward mobility, and not only towards quality of opportunity but also towards the quality of social status. This is as it should be. The outlook for educational reform is bleak unless it is linked with realistic programmes of economic and social reform. It is also important that reforms should be not just short-term tactical gimmicks but long-term strategic plan for comprehensive but realistic and pragmatic programmes.

7

ACTION SOCIOLOGY IN NORTH-EAST INDIA

A.C. SINHA

This small note on action sociology is prepared specially for a group of committed activists who, moved by the oppressive social inequality, have taken to action programme. This paper is divided into two parts, part one briefly traces the travail of action sociology and its various shades and makes a plea for a sociology of dependence. Part two informs us of the disturbing scenario for the North-East frontier region of India. This region has largely been outside the purview of the oppressive Hindu caste disabilities. Even the hierarchical structure in the Assamese plains is qualitatively different from that of the other parts of the country. With the extension of the administration to the hills a number of urban centres have sprung up during the past 150 years or so. And along with them reached the social and occupational disabilities to the hills from the plains. The glaring example is provided by the *safaiwalas* in the region, which we propose to examine briefly as a case study. There can be some other communities, groups and occupations, which may substitute for them in the region. We have exerted to link up sociology of dependence to that of the fate of the *safaiwalas*. And lastly, as applied and action expertise were largely developed and used in anthropology, we have heavily drawn from anthropology. This has been done on the ground that even if sociology is substituted with anthropology in our treatment no damage will be caused to the argument pursued here.

Sociology as an academic discipline emerged as an intensely human expertise. Broken families, neighbourhood fracas, urban violence, ethnic maladjustments, racial conflicts, etc., prompted Park and Burgess to uncover the social profile of Chicago metropolis. And that is how Chicago School of Sociology came to represent the premier trend of the discipline. On the other side of the Atlantic Emile Durkheim envisaged that the increase in population with its increasing density led to an intensification of the struggle for life. In case all members of an expanding society perform the same functions, possibly they would not produce the means of subsistence. When they are engaged in different occupations, they may exist side by side without an intensive struggle and with greater opportunity to obtain their means of subsistence. And thus an increase in the density of population leads to an increase in the division of labour.

It is evident from the above two earliest traditions that sociology was literally called to the street to confront with alive social aspects. It might have been suicide groups, social control, street corner gangs, mobs, crowds, or any other societal aspects, sociology came forward with an explanation. Thus, besides a body of theories, concepts and methods, sociological tradition also created an amount of social awareness. At times sociologists were required to contribute to solving certain emergent social problems. And that is how "social engineering" was coined as a technical diffusion of technological assistance on the part of the sociologists to underdeveloped regions and the underprivileged sector of humanity.

Sociology was born as a social science in the 19th century western urban-industrial world. That was the age of scientific inventions and geographical discoveries. The then academic atmosphere was surcharged with an air of scientism. Thus, theories, concepts and methods of sociology were demanded to be objective, neutral and value-free. Subsequently, a type of academic division of studies developed in which urban industrial studies, conducted by the scholar in his own society through the survey method, came to be known as sociology and a similar academic exercise through participant observation on a distant, exotic and tribal world of "other culture" was labelled as anthropology. Though some exceptions can be found in both the cases to the above, peasantry, which was neither urban-industrial nor exotic, distant and tribal, was the domain of both the disciplines. Those were the days of empires, when the larger part of the world was under the colonial yoke. Thus till mid 20th century sociology and anthropology like other social sciences were the preserves of the white Western countries. In this context, one may be reminded of the Indian situation in which both the disciplines taken together were taught in less than half a dozen universities prior to 1947.

The colonial powers commissioned the expertise of sociologically trained experts to solve the administrative problems in their colonies. A number of anthropologists were appointed as official aid to the administrators in Nigeria, Gold Coast (Ghana), Sudan, Rhodesia (Zimbabwe), South Africa, East African colonies, Pacific Islands, Australia, etc. In this context, the role of the International African Institute in the development of applied anthropology cannot be ignored (Mair, L.P.: 1957: 11). Similarly, the Indian Reorganization Act, 1934 in the USA envisaged establishment of the Applied Anthropology Unit to advise the office of Indian Affairs on (i) the establishment of self-governing bodies, (ii) settlement patterns on new lands acquired under provisions of the Act; (iii) programmes for the improvement of morale; (iv) policies on education; and (v) utilization of existing institutions for economic rehabilitation and social control (Barnett, E.H.G.: 1956: 37). Thus, anthropologists, as also sociologists were appointed to advise the administration on human problems, as medical doctors, botanists, geologists, engineers and agronomists as an extended administrative machinery.

Ultimately a distinct branch of applied anthropology came to be recognized as the "applications of anthropological knowledge to meet the needs of the group for which the anthropologist is working. This may include giving advice, administration or giving instruction" (Winnick: 1948: 28). There were a number of presuppositions behind the above proposition. Among them mention may be made of the following: anthropologists' expertise is as objectively applicable to social situations as that of a medical doctor; anthropological subject matter — human material — remains basically the same in most of the cases; and their advice will be compulsive. However, there are general limitations of anthropological expertise like any other social science:

(a) social scientists experience difficulty in locating tnose policy-makers where area of influence corresponds to their own area of competence;
(b) there is no vehicle on the policy-making side to transıer knowledge from the social scientist to the policy-maker; and
(c) the researchers do not have a sufficient say in the selection of problems that the client wishes to solve, and in the presentation

of the results of the research to those whom it concerns (Chern, A.B. *et al.*: 1970: 63).

The opinions differ on the above presuppositions and, accordingly, it was felt that the nature of the assignment was not alluring enough for a challenging career for many of the academicians. Thus a number of similar academic specialities were claimed such as development anthropology, consultant anthropology, policy anthropology, action anthropology, sociology of dependence, etc., a rather confusing situation. In such a situation Foster advised his co-workers: "The anthropologist should do basic research and publish articles and monographs to be read and used by administrators as they see fit. The anthropologist must serve as a short-term consultant as they see fit. The problems, but he suggests no policy, passes no judgement and fights to maintain his independence. He is here his own boss, he does not have to worry about policy, he can be impartial" (Foster: 1961: 248).

Against the above stand, action anthropologists consider themselves as "catalyst" and their concern as "participant intervention". Their major role is to develop and clarify goals; helping the community and learning something in the process. Their most influential spokesman, Sol Tax, clarifies, "An action anthropologist does not exert an undue influence or power; he would only discuss and not make decisions. Rather the members of client system would make decisions based on the alternatives thrown open to them". (Tax, S.: 1951: 58). For him the most appropriate role of an anthropologists is that of the educator, though he could be facilitator, resource coordinator, but he must not assume a position of power. As a scientist, he could not choose either the State represented by the government, or the tribe (the community), whose very existence was at stake. He was committed to realization and process for which *empathy* is the key word. Related to it are a number of action-oriented and ideologically involved practices. Radical anthropology is self-conscious movement, while committed anthropology proposes to work for diminishing the influence of States and building a humanitywide community. The radical brand seeks to ally itself with the oppressed. Naturally the radical and committed brands of academics are linked with Marxism (Sinha A.C.: 1985: 282).

The above shades of opinions amount to deeper involvement on the part of the academics. For that there are genuine apprehensions. Such a commitment and involvement may lead the academics devoting more time to bureaucracy than to the cause of the people and the study. To us this entire argument is misplaced. Its origin lies in the scientism of sociological studies which were fashioned in an atmosphere of science, technology and industry and exported to the colonies. A number of scholars believe that it is impossible for the social scientists such as sociologists to be objective, neutral and value-free. Undoubtedly when the social system is unequal, oppressive and devoid of sensitivity, sociologists have to plead for and participate in action. In recent years action anthropology is being replaced by a more radical approach known as sociology of dependence, which was used and applied in the Peruvian context. "This approach interprets Peruvian social structure in terms of multiple and inter-related chains of dependence between persons and groups of unequal power, wealth and status. These chains converge at the apex into the nation, and beyond it, the international ruling oligarchy as the structure of control is extremely centralized. Peruvian social structure is conceived as a multiple of binary relations of dependence and domination based on behalf of a dozen or so inter-related dimensions. Besides centralization and inequality, these relations of dependence and domination are characterized by the fact that the closer one approaches the bottom of the pyramid, the more atomized and marginalized people are to national life; conversely, as one approaches the apex, the better connected and integrated the organs of domination" (Van Der Berher, P.C.: 1975: 73-74). This is the stand keeping in view the demands of radical, relevant and committed sociology.

Mann pleads for commonality of approach and methods in sociology (anthropology) in case the practitioners desire to promote the creation of change in the existing social order. He sounds a warning, "Else, the fraternity of anthropologists might largely remain unacceptable to the mighty administrators, bureaucrats and policy-makers. In any case, anthropologists cannot establish their claim of being helpful in programmes of change, development and policy resolving, unless they assert to create a theoretical level and find at a practical level place for them at certain levels and in specific style of administration" (Mann, R.S.: 1986: 19). It is a fact that social scientists can play meaningful roles only when they continue to remain committed to the basic tenets of their discipline. This is also imperative for them not to sit back in their cozy academic comfort, away from the sweat of the common man. In fact, one may not necessarily participate in the eye-catching action-theatres and dramatic situations such as revolutions in the neocolonial countries. One just has to look around and join the common crowd in society in their efforts to live with dignity, work with pride and earn with honour.

II

The North-East region of India comprising Assam, Arunachal, Meghalaya, Manipur, Mizoram, Nagaland and Tripura is topographically, demographically, culturally, historically and even socially different from other parts of the country. The region, specially the Hill States, does not fit in the all-India pattern of pollution-purity syndrome of caste structure. In the plains of Assam one finds some semblance of occupational castes. However, their *khel* (hamlet unit), *mel* (age-set groups) and *pyk* (obligatory occupational squads) system of work organization were more close to a secular division of labour, Edward Gaite records in his famous history of Assam.

Musalmans, Morias, Doms and Haris were forbidden to wear their hair long and the members of the two latter communities were further distinguished by having a fish and a broom respectively tattooed on their forehead' (Gaite, E.: 1984: 242).

The hill region did not have large human settlements much less an urban centre. With the advent of the British in the region as the colonial matters around 1840, a number of urban centres such as Cherapunji, Shillong, Tura, Jowai, Kohima, Mokokchung, Aizawal, Diphu, Lungleh, etc., sprang up. These were largely administrative outposts within the tribal communities.

These tribal communities were equalitarian in the sense that nobody suffered disability because of the vocations one pursued. In fact, there was very little of specialized work itself. In such a situation, when these administrative centres were established, the colonial functionaries, used to certain level of ease and comfort, brought a number of service castes from the distant plains to serve certain specific needs. That is how washermen, barbers, shoe-makers, *safaiwalas*, tailors, butchers and other service occupationals were brought in the picture.

Shillong, the capital of composite Assam, was established as an administrative town in 1874 in the heart of the undulating Khasi Hills. It was a small administrative, missionary, educational and recuperating outpost, where civic amenities were minimal. Slowly but steadily, with the growth of town, specialized works were required. Thus, bakers, masons, plumbers, carpenters, shoe-makers, butchers, washermen, barbers and other occupationals came in the picture.

In the same context the *Safaiwalas* popularly known as *Sardars*, the *Mazhabi Sikhs*, were brought to Shillong from distant Punjab some 70 to 80 years back. They work as the municipal cleaners for the public buildings and installations and private scavenging in the individual households. In the past, they went on strike against the municipal administration. The Government brought some Kabui Nagas from Imphal to work as their substitute but the *Sardars* drove them away. Since then they have monopoly over the municipal scavenging work at Shillong. All these *Sardars* are related to each other. They maintain a close contact with their native villages, in the district of Gurdaspur in Punjab. They own some property there and frequently visit their kinsmen in Punjab. They are settled in two Municipal colonies at Bara Bazar and Goralines, have their own community Panchayat and maintain their *Gurdwara* separate from the one for other more affluent Sikhs in the town. Some of them have shaved off their hair and discarded their turban and other insignia of their religion and even some of them visit the local Christian Church. Though they have been in the town for decades there has been very little occupational mobility. Some 10 years back, we found only one male member of the community, who was employed in the white-collar job as a teacher.

Traditional practice of street cleaning has been a community affair among the various communities of North-East. Since the houses were built on the stilt, night-soil was simply dropped at the point for the natural scavengers such as pigs, dogs, etc. When a rudiment of urban centres emerged, the individual households would have their toilet pits dug in their kitchen gardens which could be moved as required. When the municipal institutions were instituted, they began hiring, *Sardars* (Sikhs or the contractual gang leaders) for cleaning the streets and toilets. These persons were invariably non-tribal plainsmen. There were individuals from the tribes such as Kabuis in Imphal and Aos in Mokokchung, who were hired for scavenging work. They took up the job just as another profession. In fact some of them moved to other occupations without any social disability. We would like a point to be noted here that with extension of a plural social base, status inequality has also been extended to the region, where such situations were not in existence in the past.

Possibly civilizational status of a community can be gauged by the measures it takes in sewage disposal, overall toiletry and cleanliness practices. So far dignity of labour is concerned, all socially relevant work should be considered equal. One may learn a few lessons from the tribal communities of Nagaland, if one wants to. Even if an Ao is engaged in scavenging work at Mokokchung, he does not suffer from any disability. He is accepted as an equal member of the community and he can easily change his vocation as and when he decides. However, a disturbing trend is extending to the hill regions of the North-East in this land of social egalitarianism, practices pertaining to sewage disposal and associated social disabilities are permeating and vitiating the social situation. When the action sociologists propose to undertake rehabilitation schemes for the *Safaiwalas* in other parts of the country in the earnest, it will be a befitting strategy to prevent this social cancer from spreading to the hills, where it has been traditionally absent.

REFERENCES

Bernett, E.H., *Anthropology and Administration*, Row, Peterron and Co., New York, 1956.

Chern, A.B. *et al.*, *Social Science and Government Policies and Problems*, Tavistock Publications, 1970.

Foster, G.M., *Traditional Cultures and the Impact of Technological Change*, Harper and Row, New York, 1961.

Gaite, E., *A History of Assam*, L.B.S. Publications, Guwahati, 2nd Edition (Reprint), 1982.

Mair, L.P., *Studies in Applied Anthropology*. Atherton Press, London, 1957.

Mann, R.S., "Conceptual Contradiction Applied Anthropology", *Man in India*, 1986.

Sinha, A.C., "Contextual Impasse and Theoretical Lead in Anthropology", *Man in India*, Vol. 65 (3), 1985.

Tax Sol, "Acculturation in Americas", *Proceedings and selected papers of XXIX International Congress of the Americanists*, Illinois, 1951.

Van Der Berghe, *Social Problems of Change and Conflict*, (ed.) M.G. Smith, Chandler, San Francisco, 1975.

Winnick, C., *Dictionary of Anthropology*, Peter O'wen, Ltd., 1948.

8

PLANNED SOCIAL INTERVENTION AND ITS SOCIOLOGICAL PREREQUISITES

T.N. VALUNJKAR

The Constitution of India guarantees the people of India three fundamental rights: justice, equality and freedom. The day when our nation adopted the Constitution marks a new chapter in the process of social development. It shows our firm resolve to bring about a peaceful revolution through constitutional means in the traditional social structure of our society characterized by social, economic and political inequalities. The adoption of the Constitution was not a political accident but represents a culmination of socio-cultural renaissance which began with the British rule in Indian Society. From Raja Ram Mohan Roy, the pioneer social and religious reformer to Mahatma Gandhi, the Father of the Nation, we witness a gradual social awakening on the part of our country's intelligentsia and growing commitment to modern egalitarian social values. Contradictions between the new egalitarian social aspirations and inegalitarian nature of our society became glaring and it was soon realized that unless radical transformation in our traditional social structure is brought about, our social aspirations would remain a lofty dream. As a result we witness the emergence of a galaxy of social reformers actively engaged in the task of upliftment of the weaker sections of our society mostly comprising the lower castes who were once untouchables and the tribal and semi-tribal communities.

It is well known that the institution of caste is the major source of social, economic and religious inequalities. The notion of ritual purity occupying a central place in the caste system created a leisure class at the top who refrained from doing any kind of manual work, and a class of menials and bonded labour at the bottom who were not permitted to undertake any activity other than ritually polluting menial work. Evil effects of such a system were delimited by the geographical isolation of the village community during the pre-colonial days. Ironically, however these evils started assuming alarming proportions with the introduction of industrial capitalism during the British rule. Thus, we see a contrasting picture on the national scene which shows the development of lofty social ideology on the one hand, and greater degradation of the under privileged sections of society, on the other. No wonder the leaders of the weaker sections of our society such as Dr. B.R. Ambedkar dedicated their lives to the task of creating social awakening for human rights among the masses and the responsibilities of the upper castes towards them. Framing of the Constitution represents culmination of this process of social awakening.

The Constitution provides the legal framework for realizing the new social aspirations and provides direction to planned social action by classifying legitimate means and goals from those that are treated as disruptive of social order. It also sanctions implicitly rearrangement in the existing social structure and consequential disturbance in the existing social structure. But the new aspirations can be realized only if the agents of change—individuals and organizations—undertake action in the form of social intervention. Without this, social values enshrined in the Constitution will remain only pious goals. Hence it may be said that planned social intervention by individuals and organized groups is a logical corollary of the great hiatus between the social values enshrined in the Constitution and the traditional social structure of Indian society. Failure to initiate planned social action would undermine the legitimacy of the Constitution.

II

A look at various programmes of planned social interventions initiated by various voluntary organizations in Indian society would reveal that they are mainly aimed at enabling the downtrodden sections of our society to achieve economic and social equality.

It is generally seen that poverty and inferior socio-ritual position in the caste hierarchy go together and they are normally group attributes. Techniques of production shifted to subsistence agrarian economy are attempted to be replaced by modern scientific techniques. In situations where this is not relevant as in the case of a great number of occupations followed by the former untouchable castes supportive occupations like dairying, tailoring, gardening, etc., are introduced among them. All these programmes aim at augmenting the meagre income of the poor families by making available to the weaker sections resources to follow the existing occupations practised by socially more advantaged communities in our society or by introducing new occupations amongst them. These measures are likely to bring about change in the existing system of social stratification and thus are potentially disruptive of existing social equilibrium.

The thrust of the second category of measures is on improving the socio-ritual status of the weaker sections. Thus, under the leadership of Dr. B. R. Ambedkar the Mahar community, the former untouchable caste in Maharashtra, adopted the programme of giving up the practice of carrion-eating, and scavenging, in a village community. These programmes created economic hardships to poor Mahar families but they were enforced by the leadership of the community with a view to improving the social status of the community. This movement met with resistance from the upper caste members as it disrupted their ritual life, and half-hearted acceptance from the poor Mahar community as they had to face considerable economic hardships. These implications of social intervention have to be taken into account by social reformers and organizations. It is essential while implementing any action programme to see that the implementation is not done in social isolation but in its structural context.

III

The structural context of any social custom or a behaviour pattern that is felt to be obnoxious and morally degrading involves linkages of such a custom or pattern with the local power structures, economic structures and socio-ritual hierarchy reflected in the caste systems. Legitimacy of such a social structure rests on the foundation of a belief system and fundamental values. We may consider the practice of carrion-eating in its structural context. Carrion-eating reinforces the lowest position of the untouchable castes as they continue to remain in a perpetual state of impurity. It also implies lowest position in the economic structure, as the untouchables are required to follow those occupations which receive so low rewards that they are not sufficient to buy even essential food articles. This also ensures supply of cheapest labour force to the upper caste people who control the means of production. The custom also enables the upper caste people to maintain their ritual purity as threats to ritual purity are warded off through such institutionalized practices. In such a situation a social action programme like abstaining from eating carrion, and not removing the dead cattle from the street affects not only an untouchable community but the entire village community. Failure to take cognizance of this social reality is likely to endanger success of the relevant action programme.

We may take another example of social action aimed at improving the economic position of the untouchable community. An attempt is made by several voluntary social organizations to improve the economic position of the untouchables by supplying them milch cattle. Improvement in the economic position of the weaker sections through such an action programme liberates them from the position of servitude and enhances their bargaining power in the village economy. This disturbs the power structure and also the system of social stratification by giving rise to status inconsistency. Such a situation triggers a movement on the part of the lower caste towards status improvement through the process of sanskritization. This shows that welfare programmes aimed at improving economic conditions of the weaker sections activates the entire network of social relationships. Unless social reformers and organizations bear this in mind social action programmers would meet with resistance from the affected groups of people. Hence successful implementation of any action programme requires prior analysis of the structural context of the social pattern intended to be abolished.

Our analysis so far has made it amply clear that there is a need to adopt systemic approach to planned social intervention. Atomistic approach to planned social action based on the utilitarian logic and monocausal concept of social change is less likely to bring about a durable social transformation. We may illustrate this point by taking one case of planned social change from Maharashtra. A programme which provided permanent houses to a wandering community of Gosavi who traditionally lived in tents was implemented with the assistance from the welfare agencies. But the Gosavis refused to occupy newly constructed houses because of the religious belief that a Gosavi should not have a permanent residence and he must keep on wandering from place to place and live in tents. The scheme was obviously based on the premise of individualistic rational orientation common in the urban community, as a universal characteristic of human behaviour. Among the Gosavis, on the other hand, decision-making was a collective process. Major decisions involving possibility of change in the traditional pattern of behaviour were taken in the caste council by the religious head. Failure to take cognizance of this structural context resulted in the resistance on the part of the Gosavi community to the new scheme of housing planned for their benefit. The deadlock was, however, overcome by a skilful approach adopted by a dedicated social worker belonging to a Scheduled Caste community who was familiar with their socio-religious ethos. He used the traditional channels of communication and decision-making to convince the members of this community to occupy newly constructed houses.

The above analysis shows how essential it is to adopt a systematic approach in planning a programme of social action. It is not just enough to provide material facilities like housing or a well but it is also equally important to understand the structure of power and decision-making. A programme of consentization is a prerequisite.

V

An act of a social intervention alters the flow of scarce resources in a social system like various kinds of facilities and rewards. In a general way it may be said that any programme of social intervention deprives those groups occupying a higher social rank of socially valued resources and provides benefits to those groups occupying a lower social rank. This social intervention creates two categories of people, namely, deprived and beneficiaries. A movement like "Bhangi Mukti" aims at benefiting the lowest untouchable caste by liberating them from the inhuman task of clearing toilets by carrying night-soil, while it deprives the upper castes of ritually essential service for maintaining their superior ritual rank. The deprivation of the advantaged groups is a consequence of our efforts to institutionalize a new set of values based on egalitarian social ethos. This objective can be achieved by re-socialization of the advantaged communities to meet the demands of the changing social condition. On the other hand, the new category of social beneficiaries cannot avail themselves of the benefits unless they remove their traditional religious beliefs and values and create awareness on the part of advantaged groups about their just demands. Thus it may be said that re-socialization of the advantaged groups and consentization of the disadvantaged groups are the prerequisites of a social action programme.

VI

Programmes of social action undertaken by voluntary agencies are based on the assumption of individual decision-making. This is largely due to the fact that such programmes are initiated by urbanites for the benefit of the weaker sections of the society. The urban-bred social organizers do not always realize that among a majority of the communities belonging to the weaker sections of society decision-making assumes collective character. Every community has a council of caste elders who wield power over the entire community. Decision-making function is generally performed by this small group who wields considerable power over the members belonging to their community. These decisions are kept secret from the outsiders. Hence outsiders rarely enjoy access to the centres of decision-making. It is only with considerable social skill that an outsider can succeed in winning confidence of the decision-makers. Unless the social organizer brings about a change in the attitudes of the decision-makers the response of the community to programmes of social intervention may not be favourable.

To conclude, it may be said that the voluntary social organizations have to play a very crucial role in translating the social ideals enshrined in the Constitution into social realities. Successful implementation of action programmes requires taking into consideration the structural context of the social pattern intended to be removed from practice. This necessitates adoption of systematic perspective in action programmes. A programme of re-socialization of the socially advanced groups and similar programmes of consentization of the disadvantaged section of society is a prerequisite for bringing about a durable change in the desired direction.

9

WOMEN AND SHUDRAS :
Some Observations

ARCHANA SINHA and NIDHI SINHA

The two most oppressed communities in Hindu society are the women and the Shudras. Their woes permeate Indian history. Kings have come and gone, dynasties have risen and fallen, empires have been built and have vanished, but these two groups have suffered through the ages, and are continuing to suffer. They have now arisen and are a challenge to our democratic Constitution. If women have been a hand-maid, a property, an object of passion and lust, the Shudras have been the communal slaves of the caste Hindus and, subsequently, of all others who settled in India with a stamp of superiority. Panikkar says, "The slave at least was a chattel of the master and, therefore, he stood in an individual relation to his owner". Consideration of economic self-interest and human feelings modified the barbarism of personal slavery. But even these mitigating factors did not apply to the system of untouchability, which was, it could be seen on examination, a system of communal slave-holding. Instead of an individual owning slaves, each village held the untouchable families attached to it in a kind of communal slavery. "Not alone villages; even the towns offer the same spectacle", Gandhiji once wrote about Vile Parle suburb of Bombay which was inhabited by well-to-do people and which was served by a flourishing municipality. "The scavengers are accommodated in quarters where there are no roads, no arrangements for water supply, and sanitary conveniences. The land itself is low-lying. The huts are hovels constructed from dilapidated tins which were once used for conservancy work. There is no lighting. Nearby is the dumping ground for the suburban rubbish which gives an eternal stench. . . . It is in these surroundings that the scavengers have to pass their life. These quarters are surrounded by fields which are often under water, breeding mosquitoes, harbouring scorpions, snakes and field rats". What is true of Vile Parle is true of any suburb or a town anywhere in India, whether it is Calcutta, Madras, Srinagar, Delhi or Patna. This is also true of the holy places of our country. The living conditions of the rural poor, and economically depressed people are no better. The so-called residences of the Shudras in the villages are secluded and segregated from those of the high caste men. It is this universal sight in India which pained Shri Jagjivan Ram extremely and made him emphatically assert at the Vidarbha Backward Classes Conference about the springing up of numerous Harijan colonies all over the country. "This is nothing but policy of segregation. They are being set up in separate colonies because the upper classes would not suffer their presence near their dwelling places. Segregated colonies are being ingeniously devised for permanent ostracism of Harijans" (*Hitawada*, 1959).

Segregation of the Shudras is, indeed, ruthlessly complete. Instead of a healthy re-adjustment in society in the wake of Independence and a democratic government, the maladjustment has come to stay, without any real remorse in the people who talk loudly about quick social reformation. The cruelty has breached all boundaries of civilised living and has surpassed in severity the racial segregation of the world. Now it is a recognised fact that the Harijans occupy the lowest and the loneliest position in the social scale (Shivam: 1960). A discussion of the Shudras leads us to another strange fact – their denominations. As the Savarnas have pedigrees, one higher than the other, the Shudras are categorised into classes, one lower than the other (Prasad, N.).

The invasion of foreign races, e.g. the Pathans, Mughals, French, Portuguese, Britishers were additional shocks to the already disturbed equilibrium of the Hindu society. Desire for personal safety led men to opportunism. Divide-and-rule, the political doctrine of the the British, drove the last nail into the coffin of the Hindu social structure. The one single factor leading to these conditions has been the formation of innumerable myths about caste superiority. But even prior to foreign invasions nine centuries ago the last word of the myth was written by Manu, in *Manusmriti*, and women and the Shudras were condemned for ever. It is this continued mental slavery which has denied the Harijans and the women the pride of life the sense of self-respect and self-sufficiency and consequently the power to resuscitate themselves. The effect of such venomous myths has been so strong that all the pious teachings of the reformers from the 16th to the 19th century has cut no ice with those who consider oppression a matter of divine right. Prof. T.K. Ommen rightly says, "The central tendency in Hindu society was that the *jatis* in the twice-born *varnas* were the value-givers, norm-setters and institution-builders and others followed them" (Ghurye, G.S.: 1950).

We have a glorious galaxy of social reformers like Raja Ram Mohan Roy, Dayananda Saraswati, Ishwar Chandra Vidyasagar, Gandhiji and so many others, to mention only a few in this regard, who positively helped the Shudras and women. The magnificent efforts of nationalist leaders like B.R. Ambedkar, N. Sanjeeva Reddy, K. Kamaraj, and Jagjivan Ram and many others who saved Indian nationhood from disaster cannot be overlooked. Their tremendous efforts cannot be ignored. However, the malaise has persisted, reflecting its deep roots. An example: In the Rajya Sabha, information was given by one Hon'ble Member "that in a certain cotton mill in Ahmedabad, no untouchable was even appointed in the weaving department as the yarn had to be sucked by mouth into the bobbin and none would suffer to be defiled by the association of a Shudra (Ommen: 1984). This is a shameful example of exclusion. Retaliation is, therefore, on the increase. Now, as consciousness about rights is dawning upon the depressed and the neglected, they are uniting to oppose their arrogant oppressors. The long course of maladjusted social behaviour has taken away conscience from both, humanity from the upper classes and self-respect from the Shudras. Now the only solution is that the upper class should confess that they have heaped poverty, illiteracy and social disabilities on their down-trodden brethren and sisters and sincerely remove the disadvantaged as quickly as possible and undertake pious atonement.

Some people with a philanthropic vision made sporadic efforts to meet the needs of these persons as they understood them. Under their leadership voluntary effort was kept alive. There was, however, no definite comprehensive plan behind this action. Some knowledge of the needs, availability of funds and desire to do something for the suffering humanity seemed to be the important consideration. But in the absence of trained personnel and a scientific approach these institutions and organizations just carried on. What is required is judicious integration of these efforts by Action Sociologists with a view to securing the Indianization of the welfare measures in spirit, in philosophy, in methods, in techniques and organizational structure.

The role of Action Sociologists is important in these directions in our opinion. The crumbling of the old order, absence of new healthy substitutes and confusion in transition have made the situation extremely complicated. Even today, a new child in the family is considered one more mouth to feed but two more hands to work. The result is that the number of needy persons is increasing enormously. Since India is a typical Third World region, frequent famine and drought further aggravate problems. These conditions should also be given due place in our thinking.

Action research for the uplift of the downtrodden through a participatory process is the need of the hour. For direct involvement of sociologists and active social workers in the process of development and also for a solution of the practical problems, action strategy and models suited for specific problematic areas have to be developed. Basically they have to plan a strategy to fight for the rights of the Shudras and suffering women. Their social, educational, financial, ecological and environmental conditions have to be improved.

The selection of the priority areas is essential. To protect the downtrodden from all kinds of hazards should be the target. There is a need to emphasize positive and preventive services. A comprehensive and rational policy solidly based on objective fact-finding has yet to be evolved.

The existing constitutional and legal provisions with respect to women and Shudras are fairly adequate with a few exceptions. But how many are aware of them? Even those who are educated are incapable of utilizing them. The processes are so complicated. It is the implementation of the same which has remained far from satisfactory. This can also be an area of operation by sociologists and reformers in the field.

While it is important to keep abreast of action programmes for the resolution of similar problems in the West and benefit from such experience, it is equally important to avoid the temptation of following Western methods of care without due recognition to local differences. This tendency of uncritical imitation has occasionally resulted in establishing services for which the bases of need and the distinctively Indian way of responding to the need have not been adequately appreciated.

Research in Action Sociology has been extremely scanty in our country. Intelligent planning and efficient utilization of available resources would demand a much better attention to research. There is an urgent need to step up and improve the training programmes for action personnel.

REFERENCES

Gandhi, M.K., "My Soil's Agony" quoted in *For Workers Against Untouchability,* Navjivan Pub. House, 1933, 17-18.

Ghurye, G.S., *Caste and Class in India,* Popular Book Depot, Bombay 1950.

Hitavada, Vidarbha Backward Classes, conference, Nagpur, Reported by Staff, June 5, 1959.

Leuva, P.T., *Rajya Sabha Official Report,* the Untouchability (Offences) Bill, 1954, Sept. 17, 1954.

Ommen, T.K., "Sources of Deprivation and Styles of Protest, the Case of the Dalits in India", *Contributions to Indian Sociology,* Sage Pub., New Delhi, Beverly Hills, London, 1984, p. 51.

Panikkar, K.M., *Hindu Society at Crossroad,* Asia Pub. House, Bombay, pp. 27-32.

Prasad, N., *The Myth of the Caste System,* Sanjana Prakashan, Patna.

Sivan, K.S., *Scheduled Castes in India, Social Welfare in India,* Publication Division, Government of India, 1960.

10

CASTE CONFLICT AND VIOLENCE

M.Z. KHAN

Caste in India, as a sociological phenomenon, has evoked much interest. Depending upon their background and perspective, writers have viewed it from different angles. To illustrate, Dumont (1970) regards caste as an ideological system, Furnivall (1939) as cooperating parts of a social whole, and Sherring (1974) as promoting cleanliness and order. Having to do with descent, occupation and rituals, the system is all-encompassing (Beteille: 1965), and its values and institutions influence all other inter-personal and inter-group relations (Sharma: 1980). It represents a multilinear tradition creating differentiated groups and subgroups, and orchestrating them into a larger whole. Nevertheless, this does not necessarily imply cultural fragmentation or social alienation but, on the contrary, cohesion and abidance.

The Indian tradition has several distinctive features (Singh: 1973) and the foremost among them is hierarchy. In a way, the philosophical relationship between *atman* (soul) and *parmatman* (eternal soul or God), the theory of *Karma* (religious duty) and the concept of the transmigration of soul — all contribute to and reinforce the inherited and ascriptive *varna* or caste hierarchy. Through the allocation of status (Ghurye: 1950), caste defines the role of the individual, singly and collectively, coming down through the ages, caste hierarchy is so well defined, imbibed and acted upon as to make caste a closed system (Hutten: 1963). As a logical corollary, achievements of an individual are mediated solely by his caste. This social reality circumscribed by institutionalized inequalities doubtless has all the makings of a conflict situation.

It goes without saying that the caste system has a bearing on the ownership and control of economic resources as also on opportunities.

Earlier it used to be almost exclusively the members of the upper castes who owned primary resources, and those of the lower castes who worked for them. Likewise, the former monopolized all the prestigious and renumerative jobs and trade and commerce. As would be readily seen, the caste system provided openly for an inequitable social order. As would be expected from these exploitative and even oppressive conditions, conflict was embedded in the social structure itself.

Moreover, earlier on, collectively upheld and accepted caste values and norms used to legitimize coercion and violence against those scheduled caste and tribe persons who would resist caste norms and inequalities flowing from them. The inequalitarian social structure also made it easier: they had no share in political power whatsoever. Upper caste persons had all the opportunity to enforce their will on the entire range of intergroup relationship (see also Weber: 1948), resorting whenever needed, to the ultimate in power, namely violence (Mill: 1956). Interestingly enough, it was not the majority inflicting coercion and violence upon the minority, rather it was the other way round, if present-day population estimates are any indicator.

Furthermore, in ancient and medieval times, notions of innate superiority-inferiority, approved and sanctified by the caste system, had brought about a criminal justice system which was essentially uneven: the manner of handling as well as the quantum of punishment would vary with the caste of the crime-doer and that the crime victim. For instance, a Shudra killing a Brahmin would be dead by stone-pelting, whereas a Brahmin killing a Shudra was expected only to undergo self-expiation. Has the contemporary social situation in this respect undergone any significant change? Even otherwise there are observers who feel that the police in the country are yet to get rid of its colonial hangover. By and large, they continue to be insensitive to changes in the social milieu and unresponsive to public opinion, and are given to arbitrary or even extra-legal methods (Khan and Unnithan: 1984). Numerically dominated by those belonging to the upper castes, the police often adopt, it is observed, a partisan approach in civil right matters. So is likely to be the case with other sectors of the criminal justice would be a logical consequence.

While caste conflict might have existed for centuries, it has become heavily accentuated and assumed endemic proportions in contemporary times. Reasons for this are not far to seek. Popularization of education, modernization (Westernization?) of social life, and the emergence of mass media, all have combined to spread large-scale awareness among the masses including those on the lower rungs of the *varna* ladder. Besides, political independence and introduction of a democratic form of government has had a many-sided impact on the caste system. It is contended that democracy and the caste system are incompatible—of the two, only one can survive (Nehru: 1972). However, this is not what has reportedly happened (Atal: 1971). Deep-seated caste norms and values have crept into and underlaid democratic institutions and become a persistent political reality (Kothari: 1970). As a result, criss-cross caste cleavages have further deepened (Seth: 1979). On the other hand, democratization of the body politics has hightened political aspirations of different segments of society including the Scheduled Castes and Tribes, to share power. Consequently, the political calculus of the multi-party system has come to be circumscribed by caste. It may be reiterated that the upper castes do not have numerical majority, if we add to the number of the Scheduled Caste and Tribe persons those belonging to the backward classes. They thrive largely on tradition. To caste strife, agitational politics has added yet another dimension. Measures to improve conditions of the Scheduled Castes and Tribes have often been sought to be promoted or thwarted through agitations of varying magnitude, intensity and duration.

Yet another reason for the accentuation of caste conflict, ironically enough, is the economic development. Since independence, the country has gone through a massive planned economic development effort. Apart from "general growth" programmes, population-specific socio-economic programmes have been launched to bring about a speedy and equitable redistribution of resources and opportunities. Rarely have these developmental efforts been free from policy and implementation problems. This notwithstanding, these change strategies have adversely affected the economic equilibrium and exacerbated caste feelings, conflicts and violence.

Latent or open, conflict emanating from social stratification has been all along an inseparable part of social life in the country. Could it be termed as caste conflict or class conflict, howsoever underdeveloped in form of thrust (see also Desai: 1966)? From a conceptual standpoint, caste and class have much in common. Both are directly or indirectly linked with economic status and occupation. Suffering from structural contradictions, both imply social stratification and hierarchy of status. Both are characterized by group identification and attitudes — making resentment, conflict and even violence almost inevitable.

Also, there are points of dissimilarity. While caste represents a closed status group, a class is relatively open and admits of mobility. As compared with the Marxist formulation visualising a pre-revolution society as being divided into two broad groups, bourgeoisie and proletariat, the caste society is patently much more asoteric and complicated: There are more than 5,000 caste groups (i.e. caste, sub-castes and sub-subcastes), differentiated in terms of traditions, customs and rituals. While in the former, all social changes are viewed as revolutionary, in the latter, they are apparently evolutionary, leading to further strengthening of the system. In class struggle, violence is a "life force" in the hands of the working class, having a degree of justification or legitimacy. In contrast, violence in caste strife appears only to be some sort of last resort, both for the oppressor and the oppressed. It can hardly be gainsaid that class conflict aims at mitigating class differences. It is also the case with caste conflict. The critical difference between the two, however, lies in the fact that caste is delineated by religious traditions, and the basis of class is indisputably economic (see also, Bottomore: 1964). This offers a plausible approach to examine the issue in hand. Perhaps caste conflicts would be class conflicts to the extent they are triggered and precipitated by economic ends.

II

In the light of the foregoing discussion, it is intended here to look into caste violence and the causes underlying it. At this stage, a few clarifications would be in order. Violence is related to aggression, but only to an extent (see Bandura: 1974). Often viewed as a normal tendency, aggression does not always lead to violence. Buss (1961) aptly dichotomizes it: While instrumental aggression may prod one to activity or excellence, expressive aggression, in the perceived absence of castes or deterrence, may manifest itself in objectionable, disturbing or destructive forms of behaviour. At any rate, violence is an extreme form of aggression. Likewise conflict is not altogether nihilistic or necessarily a precursor of violence. In its several non-violent forms, it often plays a critical role in contending with injustice and promoting social good. Nevertheless, it drifts into violence when it transgresses socio-political norms and assumes coercive and destructive dimensions. Under certain circumstances, violence may also furnish a mechanism for conflict resolution (Coser: 1966).

What is violence? The philosophical tradition in India identifies three closely related levels of violence: thought, word and deed. Similar is about the position taken by Smelser (1962). He regards violence as generalized hostile beliefs. Nevertheless, the substantive concern here is violence in behaviour in inter-group relations. Attention may be diverted to operational aspects of violence. Langness (1972), in relation to violence in New Guinea Highland, considers it as the use of forcible means to attain goals. About the same is the view of revolutionary violence: It is directed towards the realization of certain ends and interests; and in the final analysis, it is most peaceful. Certain writers have in this regard focalized person who may suffer hurt, injury and death. Most others have gone beyond person. For instance, Pitcher *et al* (1978) view violence as non-accident physical damage of person and property. However, nearer to our purposes here is the interpretation provided by Crimshaw of ethnic violence as being "assault upon individual or his property solely or primary because of his membership in a social category" (1972).

It would not be out of place to discuss a few theoretical perspectives on violence. The underlying reason for the individual, singly and collectively, to take to violence may be frustration-aggression (Doollard *et al*: 1939). In the absence of a capacity for sublimation or adjustment, individual's frustration-aggression is likely to find expression in destructive ways. In a social situation characterized by rapid social change, individuals and groups may experience "systematic frustration" which, under a given set of circumstances, may culminate in large-scale violence. Revolutionary violence is also explained in terms of group frustration caused by the hiatus between expectation and achievement (see Davies: 1962). In relation to ethnic violence, Gurr (1969) puts across the concept of "relative deprivation". He argues that a disjunction between value expectations and value capabilities as perceived by individuals or groups spawns violence. Indeed, these postulates need to be examined in relation to caste violence in India.

Keeping these perspectives in view, official information on caste violence during 1970-80 as published by the Commissioner for Scheduled Castes and Tribes, New Delhi, has been scanned. During this period, an estimated 150,000 cases of caste conflict including 4,500 cases of homicide have come to the official notice. Among these have been taken up for analysis (a) which make for a group conflict or violence and (b) which shed light on the issue under examination, namely, economic/non-economic bases of conflict or violence. Indeed, all these violent occurrences involved Hindus (79 percent of the total population) belonging to the upper castes (Brahmins, Kshatriyas or Vaishyas, also termed, as caste Hindus), on the one side, and to lower castes (officially categorized as Backward Classes, Scheduled Castes and Scheduled Tribes), on the other. The criterion adopted in the selection of cases for the present analysis is not the gravity of an occurrence but conditions that give rise to it. Hopefully, this methodological approach would facilitate the examination of the substantive issue in a proper perspective.

III

Originally conceived as a system of "division of work" the concept of caste has doubtless economic implications. Ownership or control of economic resources, occupation and interconnected relationships in production and services are some of its main ingredients. All these economic equations, especially after the political independence of the country, have witnessed significant changes. The Constitution of free India made specific provisions for the weaker sections of population, i.e. members of the Scheduled Castes and Tribes.

With a view to bringing them up and integrating them into the mainstream of social life, they have been provided reservations in educational institutions, houses of legislature and public services. Effectiveness in the implementation of policies notwithstanding, a series of land reform laws have been framed to give tenancy rights to actual "tillers of land", to put a ceiling on land holdings, and to redistribute surplus land among the landless (Frankel: 1971). Rural indebtedness as also the related system of bonded labour have attracted legislative attention. Apart from general development effort, several schemes for the selective betterment of these population groups have been initiated. Thus, it would not take long to see that the age-old economic balance between caste groups has been shaken, necessitating readjustment and realignment. Has this been free from trauma and conflict? It has not, as would be seen from the account that follows:

1. On March 25, 1978, on account of agrarian disputes, several macabre incidents took place. As a consequence two Harijans and three other lower caste persons lost their lives and scores of

houses were reduced to ashes in two villages in Rohtas, Bihar.

2. In a village in Bhojpur district, in 1978, a *mahant* (head of a seminary) led a band of 60 musclemen to secure arbitrary and forcible eviction of Scheduled Caste persons from their residential land. They had little chance in the presence of this determined band. In the carnage that followed, four of them were killed and many more sustained injuries.
3. In 1970, prolonged disputes over land tenancy between caste Hindus and Harijans in a village in Thanjavur district came to a head. In a determined and premeditated manner, the Harijan colony was surrounded during night hours and set on fire. In the holocaust, fortytwo persons met their fiery death.
4. In 1977, Villupuram in the district of South Arcot was the scene of protracted violent clashes between caste Hindus and Harijans on account of land disputes. Soon it escalated and assumed violent proportions. About 112 Harijan houses were ransacked and damaged and eight persons were murdered in cold blood.
5. In a small village in Haryana, in 1970, some persons belonging to a Scheduled Caste wanted to dig a well to augment the supply of drinking water. Although the patch of land, the proposed site for the well, belonged to the Village Council, their intentions were not to the liking of caste Hindus. Consequently, these Scheduled Caste persons were mercilessly beaten and their houses razed to the ground.

The foregoing account brings out conflict and violence flowing mainly from the changes in land tenancy rights. Closely allied to land tenancy is the system of share-cropping. Arable land is owned by one and worked on by another. Needless to mention, most members of the Scheduled Castes and Tribes are landless or are owners of petty and uneconomical pieces of land. It is, thus, mostly they who work as share-croppers on the land owned by caste Hindus. Most certainly, exploitation and mischief are interwoven in the situation. And it is share-croppers who usually bear the brunt, as is exemplified from the following:

6. Late in 1971, some Scheduled Tribe persons in a small village in the district of Purnea, Bihar, faced the wrath of land-owning caste Hindus. The latter felt that the former had cheated them over their share in the farm yield. May be they had a point; but what seemed pointless was the severity of their reaction leading to devastation and mayhem. A frenzied mob of 150 persons attacked the tribal

village with staves and sharp-edged weapons, ruthlessly hacking 14 persons to death and injuring scores of others.

Consensual caste values and prejudices appear to have the potential to dehumanise and brutalize inter-personal and even inter-group relations. Often times, caste Hindus have resorted to wanton, unprovoked and excessive violence, in order to uphold and enforce caste norms and values. This is what is evident from the following incident in Rajasthan:

7. In 1977, in a village in Alwar district, a young lad, a Scheduled Caste, unmindful of the existential reality, planted a sappling in front of his hut. It so happened that caste Hindus had a certain claim on the tract of land including the spot where the sappling was planted. They were furious. The audacity might set a bad example. They ganged up, caught hold of the impudent young man, and chopped off his ears from the root.

Next, attention may be turned to "Iswly" where essential services are rendered by Scheduled Caste persons. Traditionally, Harijans have handled in rural areas such jobs as cleaning and sweeping, disposing of night-soil, and removing of dead animals.

Likewise, sweeper women have acted as mid-wives. At times, for their services they receive some compensation, mostly in kind, and at others nothing. On the other hand, it is unthinkable for caste Hindus to handle these chores: these are unclean and degrading and would pollute them. Of late, Harijans have also become averse to render these, they are labelled as unclean and lowly. Either way, the situation has visibly upset the economic balance in village communities, giving rise to frequent group tensions. A few examples should suffice:

8. Early in 1971, the village of Bhaisorli in Mainpuri district was surcharged with discontent and tension. Scheduled Caste persons, or to be specific, Harijans, had refused to clean the night-soil. Caste Hindus, particularly landlords, were indignant and, for quite some time, they harassed and intimidated Harijans. The issue was somehow resolved before it could take ugly turn.
9. A difficult situation built up in Varanasi, in September 1971, when Harijans refused to remove dead cattle, and told their womenfolk against serving as mid-wives. The situation turned so desperate that violence was resorted to resolve the stalemate. Caste Hindus forgathered and attacked the Harijan colony, set a large number of huts on fire and a still larger number of huts were

pulled down.

10. In 1973, a similar problem raised its head in a small village in Lucknow. For quite some time, Scheduled Caste persons were refusing to remove animal carcasses. Finding no way out, caste Hindus approached the police. Certainly the violation of legal norms: In the dispute, the police did not come into picture. However, the police assured the caste Hindus of cover-up should they take the law into their own hands. Close on heels the locality inhabited by the defiant Harijans was attacked. They were savagely beaten up and a large number of them were injured, five of them had to be hospitalized.

As mentioned earlier, rarely is the ownership or control of economic resources in the hands of lower caste persons. They work for others and, in return, they receive some compensation. Whether in cash or kind, the compensation seldom has labour market priority. In some places, it may be masqueraded exploitation, in others, an unabashed oppression. However, owing to policy shifts outlined earlier, the situation is undergoing a slow but perceptible change bringing in its wake a plethora of problems in inter-group relations. A few examples would elucidate the point:

11. In 1973, the entire village of Ramapatty in Andhra Pradesh incurred the wrath of caste Hindus. Being agricultural labourers, Harijans of the village had dared to ask for higher wages, a demand which their masters were least prepared to concede to. Exasperated by the prolonged dispute, the latter raided the Harijan hamlet and burnt down a hundred huts.
12. The case of Chauri village in Bihar was a bit different. In 1972, the landless (Scheduled Caste persons) and the landlords (caste Hindus) got locked into the dispute over the scale of wages. The landlords approached the police and passed on the names of those who were in the forefront of the wage demand. Although not directly concerned, the police obliged them by taking a partisan view of the situation. But then the situation took an unexpected turn. The Harijans, inspired by the justness of their cause, resisted the police as also the police attempt to arrest the opinion leaders. As the subsequent official report showed, the police had to open fire to control the unruly and stone-throwing mob. As a result, four persons died on the spot and 24 others sustained gun-shot injuries.

> The foregoing occurrences relate to caste conflicts and violence spawned by such economic considerations as ownership of land, wage and services. It would be noticed that a few of them were altogether free from socio-cultural traditions. Nevertheless over the years there have been cases which essentially reflect culture ethos.

For long, traditional caste norms and values have characterized the rural scene in India and, in varying degrees, subjected different population groups to multiple social disabilities and oppression. Recent social, economic and legal changes have sought to stem the trend; but their full impact is yet to come about. Furthermore, this kind of directed or imposed change in inter-group relationship has intensified the social dilemma between parity and population, between equity and ritual, unleashing several unruly forces. Conflict, antagonism and violence, often brutal violence, have taken place with disquieting regularity and ferocity. For the present purposes, it is proposed to highlight a few typical cases which underscore cultural ethos or caste values — other than those having economic overtones.

It would be recalled that in the pre-Independence period, for Scheduled Caste persons the range of civil disabilities was fairly large. There were restrictions on approach, touch, sitting together, commensalism, entry into place of worship, drawing of water from the community well, constructing a brick house, riding a horse and so on. Partly through public opinion mobilization and partly through legislation, these social disabilities or anomalies are sought to be done away with. Have we succeeded in restoring civil rights to the downtrodden? Have the legal measures not bred violence? In order to respond to these questions properly, we need to look into a few representative instances.

13. In 1970, in a small village in the district of Mehsana in Gujarat, Harijans intended to worship at the temple of goddess *Maha Kali*— rather in a big way. They organized a large procession. Upper caste Hindus did not view favourably the idea of Harijans entering the temple—it would desecrate it. The procession was intercepted and scuttled. In the process, many persons were injured, some of them seriously.
14. In June 1977, there took place, in a village in Orissa, a violent clash between Scheduled Caste persons and caste Hindus. The

issue was that some Harijan youngmen were sitting on the wooden planks meant for outsized chariots in which deities were ritually sacrificed during festivals. Would it not pollute the timber? Caste Hindus took it as open sacrilege. But the audacious youngmen would not listen; and, on the contrary, they argued. In the ensuing clash, although members of both the groups sustained injuries, the one person who lost his life belonged to a Scheduled Caste.

15. Caste Hindus in a village in Guntur district, early in 1970, were highly agitated: Scheduled Caste persons of the village had polluted the village pond by taking water from it. Armed with sticks and sharp-edged weapons, they fell upon the indiscrete non-conformists. Their *sarpanch* (caste leader) was killed on the spot, many suffered serious injuries, two of them later succumbed to their injuries.
16. In the middle of 1973, due to scanty rainfall, the "Harijan Well" had dried up in the village Ranmalpur (Surendranagar, Gujarat). Hence Harijans were forced to draw water from the community well, that is, the well meant for the use of upper castes. This was resented by the village elite. The morose flared up when Harijans approached the civil authorities who somehow listened to the complaint and initiated appropriate action. Two police constables were also posted in the village to prevent breach of peace. One night, caste Hindus assembled in strength and sweeped upon the Harijan settlement leaving behind a trail of destruction. Cash and ornaments were looted, two persons were brutally done to death and several others were grievously hurt. So intense was the mob fury that the two policemen on duty were also not spared: they also sustained injuries.
17. Scheduled Caste persons in the village of Sona Vale, in Thane district of Maharashtra, had converted *en masse* to Buddhism, (which does not recognize social categories or caste hierarchy). The fact or conversion hardly mattered with the caste Hindus—to them, they remained untouchables, nevertheless. In the summer of 1974, as the water of the well used by these newly converted Buddhists had become unfit for human consumption, they started taking water from the well used by the caste Hindus. This was impertinent, if not atrocious. Consequently, the neo-Buddhists were belaboured and more than a score of them were injured.
18. In May 1980, a marriage procession of Scheduled Caste persons

was passing through a village called Kafalta, Almora. Somehow, the bridegroom duly dressed in finery and bedecked for the occasion was in a palanquin—a customary prerogative of the bridegroom—was told to come and walk, at least through the village: members of Scheduled Castes were not supposed to ride a horse or palanquin. This touched off an argument which in no time transformed itself into a violent clash. One caste Hindu was stabbed to death. Six Scheduled Caste persons were burnt alive, and another eight of them were beaten to death.

Group violence involving Scheduled Caste persons occurs not only because of contradictions in the normative environment but also because of the fact that the they are the easy target. Occupying the bottom rungs of the socio-economic ladder, they are not able to adequately defend themselves for their doings and misdoings:

19. In 1974, in a village in Anatapur district, two young men belonging to a Scheduled Caste were caught stealing *toddy*. They were ordered to climb down, and given caustic treatment. Their hands and legs were tied round the palms and they were thrashed mercilessly to the extent that one of them died on the spot.
20. Near a predominantly Scheduled Caste village in the district of Morena, in 1973, a caste Hindu used to escort his recently married sister to his house. They were waylaid and the miscreants decamped with clothes and some minor jewellery. This triggered an overthrow of violence. Suspicion went to Scheduled Caste persons in the village. In no time, caste Hindus gathered in strength and surrounded the village. Taking the law into their own hands, they burnt 46 houses to ashes and an old woman to her death. They dispersed only when the police arrived on the scene and fired aerial shots.
21. In 1973, a police constable visited Gahalpur, a small village in Bhagalpur, mainly inhabited by Scheduled Caste persons. Some villagers misbehaved with the policeman. By the night-fall, an armed police party marched into the village. It did uphold the authority of law, but through unlawful means. The law enforcement functionaries indulged in indiscriminate assault, rape and loot.

As referred to earlier, the stoic or conciliatory attitude and behaviour of lower caste groups are gradually giving way to reassertion and even to resurgence. Perhaps their faith in the legitimacy of caste value and norms which nourished the caste system and facilitated its continuance has substantially eroded (see also Bienen: 1968). Stated differently, the oppressed when pushed over the threshold of tolerance set upon the oppressor, exemplifying that violence is contagious (Berkewitz: 1970). Indeed, this is not a general trend; only occasionally are they able to take on others, violence not ruled out.

22. In 1974, a Scheduled Caste youth was beaten to death in a police lock-up at Balaghat, Madhya Pradesh. The allegation was that he along with three others was carrying on illicit relations with a woman. As the news of his death spread, the police station was surrounded by a mob and set on fire. Two policemen eventually succumbed to their burn injuries.
23. In July-August 1978, there occurred a chain of violent incidents in the Marathwada region over the issue of renaming of Marathwada University after the late Dr. Ambedkar the well-known political leader and one of the foremost champions of the cause of Scheduled Castes and Tribes.
24. In April 1978, several violent clashes took place in Agra involving Scheduled Caste persons, upper Caste Hindus and the police. It was difficult to identity the issues, excepting general inter-group hostility. Nevertheless, four persons died, 15 suffered gun-shot injuries, more than 100 received serious stick injuries, and about 1,200 houses were damaged by large-scale arson.

It would be noted from the foregoing account that caste norms and practices, which have seemingly lost their way in urban areas, continue to maintain their hold in rural areas, almost unmitigated. Caste distinctions continue to be insisted upon by upper caste Hindus to the disadvantage of the Scheduled Caste and Tribes. Neither this insistence on upholding caste distinctions, nor the conflict or violence flowing from it, has anything to do directly with economic ends.

IV

In relation to the caste system in India, terms like flexibility, mobility and adaptability need to be examined on two different planes: Intra-caste and inter-caste relationships, and community life in urban and rural areas. Evidence converges on the fact that these terms, in the present-day context, have greater meaning for and relevance to intra-caste situations. Likewise, the operation of caste norms, practices and particularly, distinctions in urban areas is less vigorous than in rural areas. This is what is brought out by numerous studies. At any rate, it is the rigidity, exclusiveness and fixity in caste norms and practices which have been the source of many contemporary problems in inter-group relations.

Roots of resentment, conflict and violence could be easily traced to the rigid hierarchy built into the caste attempting to fit humans and human aspirations into preordained rubric, caste hierarchy becomes incompatible, especially with the contemporary socio-political environment, which adds to the feelings of "relative deprivation" (Gurr: 1969). In a way, the caste system may have socially "explosive material".

It would be difficult to attribute caste conflict and violence to variations or distance in practices, usages and rituals. Instances highlighted earlier reinforce this contention. Conflict and violence occur or recur not in the quest of basic changes in the social structure, but only to lend support to a hoary tradition.

Inter-caste relations, of late, appear to have undergone numerous and perceptible changes. Scheduled Caste and Tribe persons, having grown somewhat right-conscious, assertive and aspiring, have not only attracted violence but also in quite a few instances offered what is termed as "violence of protest" (Sharma: 1980). This swing in the social situation or "circular reaction" among these population groups may not be without meaning or purpose. To Scheduled Caste and Tribe persons, disenchanted with the normative social order as well as uncertain effectiveness of harmonizing or equalizing measures, violence may be *ultima ratio*. Their militancy or, to be precise, their counter-violence may as much hasten the pace of progressive initiatives as it may free them from primordial inferiority complex. As a spin-off, it may also lead to a better articulation of their grievances and interests. This aside, violence by lower caste groups directed against upper caste groups has an element of similarity with violence by the latter against the former: It also does not aim at basic changes in the social structure or at the mitigation of caste differences. It merely seeks a just place in society for lower caste groups.

It would thus be hasty to infer that caste conflict and violence denote class conflict, in a transformed or underdeveloped form. Indeed, a large number of conflicts occur which have economic origins or ends. But the caste system has even had economic underpinnings.

Besides, a still larger number of conflicts take place on issues arising from traditions, norms, practices and rituals. Apparently, the caste system is too deeply entrenched to allow the formation of classes or the precipitation of class conflict. What is more, caste conflict or violence, in its diverse and menacing forms, does not aim at a casteless society; rather it strives to achieve some kind of social symbiosis and to forge inter-group relations based on dignity and justice.

Caste is a distinctive and esoteric feature of Indian society (see also Weber: 1948). It may well be understood with that perspective in view. If it has outlived its utility or grown dysfunctional, it may well be accepted accordingly. An attempt to equate the caste system with class system, and caste conflict with class conflict may amount too tacit justification or legitimacy both for the caste system and caste conflict.

REFERENCES

Atal, Y., *Local Communities and National Politics,* National Publishing House, Delhi, 1975.

Bandura, A., *Aggression: A Social Learning Analysis,* Prentice-Hall, New Jersey, 1974.

Berkewitz, L., "The contagion of violence: An S-R mediational analysis of some effects of observed aggression" in Arnold, U.G. and Page, M.M.(Eds.), *Nobraska Symposium on Motivation,* Chicago, Aldina-Atherton, 1970.

Beteille, Andre, *Caste, Class and Power,* University of California Press, Berkeley, 1965.

Bienen, H., *Violence and Social Change,* Chicago University Press, 1968.

Bottomore, T., *Sociology,* Allen and Unwin, London, 1964.

Buss, A.H., *The Psychology of Aggression,* John Wiley, New York, 1961.

Coser, L.A., "Some social functions of violence", *The Annal,* 1966.

Desai, A.R., *Social Background of Indian Nationalism,* Popular, Bombay, 1966.

Davies, J.C., "Towards a theory of revolution", *American Sociological Review,* pp. 5-19, 1962.

Dollard, J., *Frustration and Oppression,* Yale University Press, New Haven, 1939

Dument, L., *Homg Hierarchicus,* Weidenfield and Nicholeen, London, 1970.

Franckel, F.R., *India's Green Revolution: Economic Gains and Political Castes,* Oxford University Press, Bombay, 1971.

Furnivall, J.S., *Netherlands and India: A Study in Plural Economy,* Cambridge University Press, Cambridge, 1939.

Ghurye, G.S., *Caste and Class in India:* Popular, Bombay, 1950.

Grismshaw, A.O., *Interpreting Collective Violence,* in Short, J.A. and Walfgang, M.E. *Collective Violence,* Alidine-Atherton, New York, 1972.

Gurr, T.R., *Violence in America: Causes and Prevention,* Aldine-Atherton, New York, 1972.

Hutten, J.H., *Caste in India,* (Fourth Ed.), Oxford University Press, London, 1963.

11

CHALLENGE OF DEVELOPMENT, SOCIOLOGY AND ACTION SOCIOLOGIST

S.N. TIWARI

Wedded to the goal of rapid socio-economic development through democratic means the Government in independent India at the Centre and in the States has adopted a package of measures to launch an onslaught against the various important problems of the country like poverty, unemployment, underemployment and others. For the sake of convenience the Government policies may broadly be put under two categories. In the first place it is assumed, under the impact of percolation or growth theory of development, that wealth must be created or increased somewhere. Since it has the natural tendency of growing faster among the upper classes of society, nothing should be done to discourage its growth there. Once it is sufficiently accumulated at the level of upper classes, it will automatically percolate to the lower strata and thus a general prosperity/development could be brought in the country. The other category includes those steps, undertaken mainly under constitutional provisions, which are exclusively meant for amelioration of conditions of the Scheduled Castes, Scheduled Tribes and other backward classes. Such measures may be put under the policy of reverse discrimination or protective discrimination. But the important problems of the country, in spite of four decades of planned development programmes, have not only remained unsolved, rather have further worsened. To quote Ashok Mitra, "One may suspend one's judgement on the issue of absolute impoverishment, but that some sections and regions have grown particularly poorer in relation to some other sections and regions and that over-all income distribution has become perceptibly more inegalitarian over the period is beyond doubt" (1975 : 1705).

For example, more loud-speaking has been practised in the context of modernization of Indian agriculture popularly called as Green Revolution. No doubt the production has increased but the conditions of the poor and needy have worsened. The Green Revolution experience in North India has disproved the percolation theory. The farm assets, instead of percolating to the lower strata over the years, have shown a tendency of being monopolized by the rich farmers. Similar had been the fate of credit societies and agencies like the SFDA. Consequently it is realized that "they (the poor) are becoming restive. Organized violence is on the increase . . . the very fabric of democracy will be in jeopardy (Minhas: 1971) and it urgently required to prevent the Green Revolution from turning into red (Sachchidananda: 1972). On the other hand, India has ample natural and human resources, it possesses a large and well-organized infrastructure of formal education, a large reserve of educated manpower and a well-developed mass media (Swaminathan: 1976).

But the fact is that development as an ideal has lost much of its magical quality. It is no longer the panacea of all ills of contemporary India. It has now become evident that the notion has poorly been defined, economic development has often been confused with development as such. Economic growth has generally been measured in terms of GNP and per capita income and that is a false indicator of development as it has little bearing on the distributive aspect of the fruit of development. And it does not significantly alter the quality of life of the ordinary people. It has become a common knowledge that an impressive rise in national income often accentuates deprivation and misery by consolidating inegalitarian structures. As a result, the hands of the exploiter and the oppressor are strengthened and the magnitude of destitution and suffering is actually increased. Such experiences are already noticed in the case of developmental efforts in India.

By tradition, sociology, by and large, has been at home in the study of *status quo* of the society and its tendency has been more towards its maintenance though with minor adjustments and modifications here and there. Radical alternatives are thought of only by a few. The discipline emphasizes its concerns to small-scale societies considering them as if they are autonomous systems. It cannot relate these societies to global forces and to the dialectic of power operating in the contemporary world. Mostly it continues to maintain a value-free posture but is uncertain about the role of sociologists in society and also about determining the criteria of the relevance of research.

Consequently its concern with analytical handling and social responsibility of socially most relevant issues such as poverty, exploitation, unemployment and population growth is feeble. A great deal of research has turned out to be the pursuit of triviality. For example, in India a wealth of data accumulated through the village studies by sociologists, social anthropologists and other social-scientists have given more emphasis to the economically prosperous segments of the small-scale village society. The large bulk of the poor and unemployed have received very little attention. However, it has been felt but by a few that the relevance of sociology lies in the area of dissent between the ideology of the ruling class as agent of values and the aspirations of the people at large (Singh: 1984). In fact our immediate task . . . is to distinguish those vulnerable regions of the social structure through which we may be able to break through the impasse and effect the stipulated course of change (Mukherjee: 1964).

It may be expected that sociologists in India should play a more decisive role and enrich the discipline with the articulation of a grassroot consciousness but largely it has not happened. Most of them have not been able to decolonize their minds either in the choice of research problems and analytical treatment or in respect of the theoretical framework and research method. Their individuality and autonomy are at stake. More or less their intellectual styles continue to be imitative and themselves alienated. Consequently they find themselves increasingly incapable to relate to the people and their society, the main concern of sociology. It is really tragic that most of the sociologists who matter in the discipline in India and other developing countries should see through Western eyes. Their writing is mainly in a foreign language and thus they communicate only within their profession. Hardly it contributes to cognitive transformations in the people studied and enlarge their consciousness. As a result, it accounts for the very limited and feeble impact that sociology has made on development in India. But this situation has started changing slowly. Some of the sociologists particularly of younger generation seek new frontiers and radical alternatives showing and involving with some of the living issues related to the general mass particularly the deprived.

Sociologists in India must take into account the problem of the inequality of development. The unequal levels and rates of development in India (consequently the rich are becoming richer and the poor poorer) are the main cause of the disharmony, dissension and discord. It should be realized that little genuine development is possible in the impoverished India if the pattern of stratification and quality of life of the common, downtrodden man are not fundamentally modified. Restructuring of the Indian Society has to be done. It is a fact that so long as inequality of power prevails and cumulative inequality is at work, access to resources is also bound to remain unequal. Persistence of extremes in the ownership of wealth reflected through affluence and low subsistence poverty is continued and so the society will experience situations of economic rootlessness, alienation and loss of human worth and dignity.

Now the need of the hour and feeling of social responsibility demand that the sociologist must act and play the genuine role of action sociologist. Continuation of cultivation of the discipline as an academic luxury must be stopped. The majority of the Indian population are weak and deprived and their interest must get the top priority and attention for the development of the nation. Here action sociologists can play their rightful role by articulating the consciousness of the deprived and the degraded. At the start such people may be socially educated by making them aware of various provisions under the Constitution and facilities provided by the Government. And they should be acquainted with the bottlenecks in the delivery system so that they could resist exploitation by the chosen few and the officials of different levels of administration. Besides they should be educated regarding the in-built mechanism of traditional stratification reality promoting inequality and other ills. All these can aid their cognitive transformation and enlargement of consciousness. To be able to do all this action sociologists will have to relate themselves organically to these groups of the weak, identify themselves with the cause of the poor and pursue their role with commitment and dedication. In other words, they should involve with the activities meant for the development of the deprived in urban or rural India. The discipline can be utilized with commitment as ideational rationale and support for major changes in the desired direction. Its social analysis and analytic potential can acquire meaning and significance only when they are relevant and are carried with creative imagination. It may help in indigenizing the discipline.

12

ACTION SOCIOLOGISTS AND DEVELOPMENT : Some Case Studies

MANOHAR LAL

Action Sociologists have a crucial role to play in the national development process. They may be called to advise on the implementation of development programmes and on the solutions to problems arising out of its implementation. They may contribute by way of evaluation of the success of particular programmes in the light of their objectives. They may also independently formulate and implement researches of theoretical interest to sociology/anthropology and/or of practical importance to the administration.

For more than a decade I have been actively associated with a number of action projects run by the Government or voluntary organizations in rural and tribal areas of Bihar. These are action programmes, integrated rural development programmes and voluntary action for tribal development. My association with various projects and programmes was in the nature of participatory intervention. All of these projects shared a common strategy of implementation of their programmes through people's action. It is this aspect of these projects which has been central to my professional interest. In the following pages case studies of four different action programmes from Bihar are reported to illustrate the significance of participatory approach to development and the scope for effective intervention by sociologists.

People's Action for Health and Population Control

This project was undertaken by the Sarvodaya Ashram, Sokhodeora, district Nawadah in the mid-seventies with an objective to work out a package of programmes for health and medical care and family welfare planning. It aimed at organizing a voluntary structure to take care of the delivery of the programme package with active involvement of the grassroot village bodies such as Gram Sabhas and Gram Panchayats. For this purpose village health committees were formed in the project area. These committees took part in fixing up the priority of the health programmes. While some of the committees remained active and did commendable job, others became inactive with the passage of time. The success of these committees rarely depended upon the sustained efforts of the convener and members possessing leadership qualities and commitment to serve their people.

People's Participation in Adult Education Programm

One of the intended outcomes of the adult education programme is the organisation of awareness groups of learners for encouraging action to bring about social transformation and improve the standard of living. In the evaluation studies conducted by me of the adult education programmes run by voluntary organisations and Government agencies during 1980-82, it was observed that learners had shown organisational capacities in solving specific problems in most of the projects under study. In one of the projects, i.e. Jagdishpur in Bhojpur district, Nehru Yuva Clubs and Mahila Clubs were created in the project village. These clubs aimed at creating social consciousness and providing a forum for sharing of village development and growth of folk culture. These clubs also held educative cultural programmes for the villagers.

In the Adult Education Programmes of the K.R. Education Association, Bettiah in West Champaran district of Bihar found it necessary to create and operate people's organisation called "Chetna Sangh" in the village itself to take up the local responsibility both for adult education and development activities related to it. Thus, along with the adult education centres, the Chetna Sanghs too were formed in each village. Superstructures such as Regional Chetna Sanghs and the Super Chetna Sanghs were also created for coordination. Chetna Nidhi or fund was raised by collections from the village and deposited in the postal savings account. This fund was used for the repairs of the village roads, provision of medical care to the destitutes of the villages, construction of huts for the helpless etc. Chetna Sanghs have also locally settled a number of land disputes, some of which had been lying in the courts for years. In one of the cases the Chetna Sangh helped the low caste people to redeem their right to worship in the village temple. It was to be noted that whether at the village or regional or super Chetna Sangh level, the selection of the office-bearers was done democratically by the people concerned themselves. The office-bearers represented not only the different areas of the village or the regions but also the different regions and castes. During evaluation it was found that some of the Chetna Sanghs had become dysfunctional over time. Many of these did not meet regularly and assembled only whenever some important issue was raised in the village.

Paru Prakhand Samagra Vikas Pariyojna (PPSVP)

This voluntary organisation has been working for integrated rural development in the Paru block of Muzaffarpur district since 1980. The programme aimed at making the people of the block self-reliant to meet their development needs over a period of seven years. The programme inputs included houses for the poor, construction of village roads, agricultural inputs, industries, production activity, education, training and cultural uplift and family welfare and organising the rural poor for development.

In the beginning of the project, village development councils, youth clubs and Mahila Mandals were formed. It was found that after some time some of these institutions became dysfunctional and inert. Some of the reasons for the failure of these organisations to take off were induction of inactive conveners and members in them, lack of objectivity and role clarity and communication gap between project personnel and office bearers/members of these village organisations. It was suggested that such organisations should have been created in a few selected villages around certain development programmes and then slowly expanded to other villages. Those villagers who would show spontaneous response and volunteer to help in implementing various programmes should be identified and trained before putting them on the job. Only a band of such committed trained and aware villagers would be able to infuse strength into village organisation to play an effective role in implementing development programmes.

Some other reasons for lack of adequate participation by the village people in project programmes were lack of experience of field workers in soliciting popular involvement, general environment of lopsidedness of governmental programmes providing very little scope for participatory development resulting in indifferent attitude of the people for any development programme. Another difficulty is that these programmes are time-bound and have physical targets to be achieved during a certain period. This leaves little time for creating awareness among the people and organise them for full participation in these programmes. Thus, these projects go ahead with concentration on physical targets and do not wait for people's readyness for participation and active involvement. Close contact between project personnel and village people can certainly create bridges between programmes and people.

Voluntary Action for Tribal Development

The Gram Nirman Mandal (GNM), Sokhodeora, undertook a programme of tribal development during 1978-1981, in a tribal village of Kowakole and Khera Blocks in a compact area. Various components of the Tribal Development Project (TDP) constituted development of agriculture, animal husbandry, drinking-cum-irrigation wells, common facility service centres and health care.

The programme was implemented by a band of project staff supported by village volunteers. A Regional Tribal Development Committee (RTDC) was constituted for supervision and monitoring of the project implementation. The RTDC constituted of tribals chosen from all the project villages. The members were selected democratically by the village people. The GNM played the advisory role. As a part of people's contribution, the labour component in construction of buildings for service centres was provided by the tribals in the form of Shram Dan.

The RTDC was supposed to meet every month to review progress of the TDP but since the beginning it had met only six times in a period of two years. Of the 11 members not all attended all the meetings. The RTDC hardly took any initiative in implementing the programme. Monitoring of the seven projects through the RTDC was very unsatisfactory. It seemed to play a passive role in the whole of the programme. It was because it had not much say in the utilization of project resources. The office-bearers of the RTDC were found to be not clear about its role and function in implementing the development programme. It did not show any initiative or assert its influence in project matters. Slowly its role was taken over by the project personnel. The members of the RTDC and other tribals perceived that the GNM rather than they were responsible for the effective execution and management of the TDP. Thus, they always looked to the GNM and the project staff for initiating any developmental action. However, once a particular activity was started the RTDC and the people came forward and participated at a later stage.

Experiences drawn from the preceding studies as well as extensive research and experience of other development scientists in recent years have shown the significance of people's help in implementing planned efforts to improve the quality of their lives. This participation includes roles for local people in assessing their needs, organising local development activities, implementing these activities, committing resources to them and assessing their impact. In general the benefits of this approach are that people tend to support and commit themselves to activities in which they feel some belongingness. In turn, such belongingness is fostered by real involvement in planning and managing these activities. Action Sociologists, through participatory intervention, can diagnose factors inhibiting people's participation, prescribe solution to it and evaluate ongoing programmes so that development programmes are planned and implemented with imagination and with better scope for people's active involvement leading them from the present state of dependence to that of development with social justice.

13

ACTION SOCIOLOGIST : Voluntary Organizations and Development: A Case Study of Samanwaya Vidyapeeth, Bagha

ANIRUDHA PRASAD

The role of action sociologists and voluntary organizations and their importance in our socio-economic life has been realized in our country from the very beginning. During the 19th century, several charitable societies were active in eradicating the evils of ignorance, disease, bad housing and sanitation, poverty, flood and drought, etc. By the early 20th century, a large number of social workers and voluntary organizations had come into existence. However, in the early thirties when Gandhiji announced his 19-point constructive programme, a large number of active social workers and able voluntary organizations emerged in different fields of social action and social amelioration. Harijan Sevak Sangh founded by Mahatma Gandhi in 1932 was the leading organization before Independence. In fact, they were organized for voluntary social service for good causes (Verma: 1969).

After Independence, the number of social workers and voluntary organizations increased rapidly. These were engaged in a variety of constructive activities aimed at uplifting the rural poor. Some have involved the general population in various kinds of social action as well as in national perspective for development. For example, the Gujarat Vidyapith which is a national university started by Gandhiji when he gave the call for the boycott of the Indian universities started by the British, its specific aim being to help in improving the conditions of the living of the backward classes through education and training. In Gandhigram (Tamil Nadu) also there is a national university which organizes a network of extension services in the villages of its surrounding areas, and fosters social action research in the same field work (Desai and Choudhary : 1977).

Some social workers and voluntary organizations are engaged in the building up of developmental infrastructure in the interior areas of the country. Some of the voluntary organizations at the national level engaged in constructive work at the local and village level are, by and large, based on Gandhian ideology. They work for village reconstruction or "Samagra Gram Seva" which means integration of the individual with the society. They develop the community spirit of self-reliance, cooperative living, mutual respect, respect for law, dignity of labour and an all-round development of the rural masses. They are engaged in strengthening the existing agencies and fostering development of new agencies in the field of socio-economic action. Sometimes, they provide assistance to their member agencies in terms of specialized expertise on material support (Desai and Choudhary, 1977).

Bihar has also a long tradition of social action and voluntary organization engaged in a variety of constructive work in the field of health, education, rural development, rehabilitation, relief, youth organization, women's uplift, sanitation, anti-untouchability, Antyodaya, and other socio-economic programmes. Some of the voluntary agencies and social workers are engaged in agricultural development, extension, irrigation, land reclamation and development, afforestation, khadi and village industries, welfare activities like houses for destitute children, formal education, protection against atrocities particularly on the Scheduled Castes and Tribes. Some social workers and their organizations in Bihar are not merely interested in relief and charity work, but they intend to inculcate new values of life by integrating education and developmental work. Although such organizations are very few, their workers are committed to establishing a new society free from exploitation and injustice.

Some organizations have been active in the rehabilitation of the Scheduled Castes, Scheduled Tribes and other weaker sections of society on Bhoodan and Gramdan land. They are engaged in reclamation of Bhoodan land. The leading organizations which are engaged in this task are Gram Nirman Mandal (Nawada), Shram Bharti and Gram Bharti (Jamui), Samanwaya Ashram (Bodh-Gaya), Sarvodaya Ashram Ranipatra (Purnia), Sarva Seva Farms, Antyodaya Samiti (Gaya), etc. However, there are some organizations in Bihar which work only among the Harijans and Adivasis. These organizations are Santhal Paharia Seva Mandal, Adivasi-Harijan Vikas Vidyapeeth, Samanwaya Ashram, Prayas, Adimjati Seva Mandal, Akhil Bharat Banwari Panchayat, Mushar Seva Mandal, and some Church agencies. In fact, these organizations are active in the upliftment of Harijans, Girijans and Adivasis in the social, educational, economic and cultural aspects of life and fight for justice by means of non-violence. Out of these organizations engaged in multifarious activities for the betterment of Harijans, Sulabh International is the only organization in Bihar, perhaps in India, which has been actively engaged in the upliftment of the scavengers for past 15 years. It has made earnest efforts in the conversion of latrines into *Sulabh Shauchalayas*. Further, it is engaged in rehabilitating the scavengers by providing them training in small trades for their livelihood.

II

In the foregoing paragraphs, we have discussed the various aspects of the role of voluntary organizations in the development of Harijans in Bihar. Here, we give a case study of a voluntary organization centred round the Mohanpur Block of Gaya district.

"Samanwaya Vidyapeeth" is one of the centres of Samanwaya Ashram, Bodh-Gaya. The Vidyapeeth is situated at Mohanpur Block of Gaya district. It has been working for the Mushahars. one of the most depressed Harijan castes. It started working among the Mushahars in 1970. The idea behind establishment of this Samanwaya Vidyapeeth was to train children from the Mushahar community in farming, to search for an alternative system of education in place of the present system of education and to train social workers from among the children for dedicated work in the villages (Prasad, 1986).

In the beginning, there was much opposition from society. The rich men in the village were against the Samanwaya Vidyapeeth. They argued "if the children of the labour class start to study in schools, who will be their *Kamia*"? They started spreading rumours that those children taken to school will be sent to other places for permanent settlement. Hence, parents of these children were also frightened. Dwarkoji, a committed social worker of Samanwaya Ashram, resisted all these attempts of the landlords and rich persons of the area. Thus, voluntary action sometimes not only becomes difficult, but it creates resentment among the people due to misunderstanding and wrong interpretation. It poses a problem for social scientists particularly Action Sociologists as to how these difficulties could be tackled.

Presently, there are 116 resident students enrolled in the Vidyapeeth. By and large, they are Mushahars. They are given practical knowledge in the field of agriculture, dairy farming, diesel machine, motor repairing, etc. In fact, here education is given to the Mushahar children in terms of knowledge, behaviour and character with emphasis on creativity which is lacking in other residential schools for the Harijans run by the government agencies. In such schools, the drop-out rate among the Harijans is higher than among other children. In making such a comparison, we must remember that the Government has made provision for special facilities such as hostels, scholarships, and free text-books for Harijan students. Despite this, the education system has failed to attract the majority of Harijan students at all levels, and fails to retain those who do enroll in the school. This is not the case with the residential schools run by the Vidyapeeth. Here the drop-out rate among the Mushahars is very negligible. It ranges between 10 and 15 per cent in the case of female students and 10 and 20 per cent in the case of male students. Here all the teaching is greatly supplemented by practical training in the fields of agriculture, dairy farming, kitchen work, etc. Here teaching is creativity oriented, not merely degree or diploma oriented. Moral education is also imparted. The Vidyapeeth has been experimenting this method among the Mushahars for the past 15 years.

The Vidyapeeth has also done excellent work in the field of rehabilitation of Mushahars in the area. It has supported about 1,000 such families in the Blocks of Mohanpur, Fatehpur and Bodh-Gaya by providing the Bhoodan land, houses, irrigation, health services, and *Balwadis* for their children. Besides, it has been playing a vital role by providing shelter to the Mushahar orphans of the area. It has helped about 20 such orphan children since its establishment. Those who had been bonded to landlords are now free from their clutches. Attitudes towards social customs like dowry, funeral feast, and the habit of drinking liquoi among the Mushahars of the area are undergoing a marked change. Now, the Vidyapeeth is paying more attention to economic programmes like demonstration on agriculture farms, horticulture, dairyfarming, crafts, village reconstruction, land development, relief services, etc. Not only that, it has been making good effort to solve the unemployment and underemployment problem among the Mushahars of the area.

Thus, Samanwaya Vidyapeeth has taken up an important role in the development of Harijans in general and Mushahars in particular. Whatever services it extends for the development of Harijans in the area is the net addition to the total development of Harijans in the country. Any new addition, however meagre, helps in pushing up development of the deprived in the country. Viewed from this point of view, the role of voluntary effort assumes great economic and social significance, particularly poverty alleviation.

REFERENCES

Desai, I.P. and Choudhary B., *History of Rural Development in Modern India*, Volume II, Impex India, New Delhi, 1977.

Prasad, A., *Samanwaya Ashram in the Service of Harijans*, Janaki Prakashan, New Delhi, 1986.

Verma, M.B., *History of Harijan Sewak Sangh from 1932 to 1968* (Hindi), Udyogshalla Press, Kingsway, New Delhi, 1969.

14

CHILD DEVELOPMENT : An Area for Action Sociology

B.B. MANDAL

The statement of Prof. R. Debre that "the child is a modern invention" (1979: 5) is very appropriate for a country like India. Children have always been with us but it was only a little over two decades ago that we have come to realize the value of children as potential human resource for the future of the nation. It was only in the Third Five Year Plan that a programme for child development was introduced under the social welfare sector. Prior to that, the Government's effort was directed mainly towards universalization of primary education and in a limited way towards pre-school education on an experimental basis. During the Third Plan two important experiments were launched to provide integrated service of education, health and nutrition to children from birth to adolescence, as well as to create a new cadre of workers called the *Balsevikas* for providing pre-primary education to deprived children of rural and urban areas. In the Fourth Plan, the scheme of family and child welfare services overtook these experiments of the Third Plan. Studies, however, demonstrated that the scheme did not get off the ground. The *Balwadis* operating under the scheme failed to provide the base even for nutrition and immunization programmes. There was not only paucity of funds but also serious lack of coordination between the officials and the voluntary workers incorporated into the management of the scheme (Mandal, 1980).

In August 1974, the Government of India proclaimed the National Policy for Children, according to which the State should provide adequate services to children both before and after birth and through the period of growth to ensure their full physical, mental, emotional and social development (Government of India: 1975). Realizing the magnitude of the problem facing the children of the country and the limited availability of resources, the programmes pertaining to preventive and promotive aspects of child health, nutrition for children below six years, care of the destitute children, day-care facilities and rehabilitation of handicapped children have been accorded high priority.

An important development that can be ascribed to the National Policy is the evolution of the scheme of integrated child development services which aims at providing a package of services to children below six years and expectant and nursing mothers. The package consists of nutrition, immunization, health check-up, referral service for children and mothers, pre-school education, recreation, health and nutrition education of mothers, family planning and provision of safe drinking water (Government of India: 1973).

II

The basic components of child development are health, hygiene, nutrition and education. The Government has envisaged and launched programmes on each of these components. These programmes have a two-fold objective. They aim to deliver services to the children, with special focus on the children of weaker sections for their physical and mental growth. The latent objective of the programmes is to create certain values which in turn can set new norms guiding child care and child development. These new norms will eventually replace those old norms which are considered outdated and dysfunctional in the context of present scientific knowledge.

In this paper an attempt has been made to ascertain whether the programmes are capable of rendering the services as well as creating the norms regarding child development in the State of Bihar or Action Sociology is required to play a role in fulfilling the twin objectives of the programmes.

III

In the State of Bihar, actual working of child development programmes such as immunization, health check-up, nutrition, pre-school education, etc., is anybody's guess. There is no aggregate information which can give a direct hint about their performance. An indirect indicator of the aggregate level that may have been, is infant mortality. But this information for the State is conspicuously absent in any Government publication for over a decade.

In fact, no body knows even the proportion of child population even after five years of the 1981 Census. However, the extent of health and medical services available in the State can be guessed from the doctor-population ratio, bed-population ratio and the per capita expenditure on medical and health services. According to the latest available data (Government of India: 1984) there is one doctor for every 4,746 persons in the State as against 3,000 in India (UNICEF: 1981). There is one bed for 5,000 population against 3,000 in India. While the per capita expenditure in the country in 1981-82 was Rs. 27.86, it was only Rs. 14.49 in Bihar (Government of India: 1984).

IV

Since the aggregate data presented above do not indicate the actual working of the programmes, it is imperative that their functioning may be seen in exact field situation. For over a decade the author has been conducting studies on the different aspects of child development. Some of these studies give ample idea of the working of the programmes.

In order to check infant mortality and morbidity, the immunization programme has been given priority. But till now, only a negligible percentage of the children has been immunized. A recent study shows that only 1.5 per cent of the estimated children in the district of Khagaria has been immunized against preventable diseases like tetanus, diptheria, whooping-cough and polio (Mandal: 1985). In numerous cases the necessary course of immunization has not been followed. A target for this is set every year but is never achieved (Mandal: 1986).

Doctors posted in the blocks are concerned for their own welfare than that of the people. They run private clinics. At times immunization of children and expectant mothers is done on payment (Mandal: 1985, 1986). They hardly ever visit the health sub-centres.

In ICDS Blocks regular health check-up is expected to be done. Doctors or health staff seldom visit the *Anganwadis*, Administrative coordination among the various departments concerned with ICDS is lacking (Mandal: 1985).

Studies show that hand-pumps have been installed in villages almost as per the set norm of 250 persons per hand-pump. But it is admitted by the concerned officials that 30 to 40 per cent of the hand-pumps are not in working condition. Most of them have not been repaired for want of funds. Primary schools are seldom provided with safe drinking water facility. Most of the handpumps do not have plastered platforms. Surface water seeps below and contaminates the groundwater. Because of all these factors, safe drinking water is hardly available to the people.

In ICDS Blocks the supplementary nutrition programme is in operation. Although the *Anganwadis* are called by the local people as "*Khichri Pakao Kendras*", nutritional diet to pre-school children of weaker sections is not given regularly, as supply of cereals is irregular. There may be doubt about the nutritional status of the children having improved but there is no doubt that the programme has proved to be income-generating for ICDS officials. *Anganwadi* workers receive as much as 20 per cent less than the fixed quota of cereals, though they are required to sign for the full quota (Mandal: 1985). The overall impact of the different programmes is that the children die of diarrhoea, dysentery, tetanus, jaundice, rickets, etc.

Education, in spite of all efforts, has not made any great stride. Even in Alauli, for example, where ICDS programme has been launched and where the pre-school children are supposed to get necessary motivation in Aganwadis for formal education, the situation is not encouraging. Only 26 per cent of the children in the school-age attend school. Reasons for low enrolment in schools are many. Poor parents do not send their wards to school as they are unable to meet the schooling expenses. They are asked to pay admission fee, examination fee, building fee, etc. (Mandal and Sinha: 1979). Many poor parents prefer engaging their children in income-generating activities to sending them for education (Mandal and Sinha: 1979, Mandal: 1985). Some poor parents think that education makes the children unfit for physical labour. As they are unable to give their children higher education, they do not want to spoil the life of their children. Girls are not given education as it is difficult to find suitable marriage partners for them. Parents are required to pay more dowry also.

Functioning of primary schools is not encouraging. In Khagaria district, for example, 23 per cent of the primary schools do not have buildings. Classes are held in open space under the trees. In certain areas, teachers remain absent for days together. At times school hours are changed to suit the convenience of teachers (Mandal and Sinha: 1979).

V

In order to derive full benefits from the programmes, it is imperative that action sociologist should act as an interventionist. The present gloomy state of affairs can partly be explained in terms of infrastructural inadequacy and inefficiency of the Government functionaries entrusted with the onerous task. But the real explanation lies somewhere else. It is the people who should be made conscious of their responsibilities and motivated about the advantage of the programmes. It is they who can put the functionaries to task. At present there is no linkage between the people and the functionaries.

The latent function of these programmes is to set certain norms which will guide the people in regard to child care and child development. These norms cannot be specific guide to action so long as these are not institutionalized. A norm is said to be institutionalized when the following four conditions are met. Firstly, a large number of people should be aware of the norms. Secondly, they should accept the norms in principle. Thirdly, most if not all who accept the norms should take them seriously and internalize them. Lastly, the norms should have sanction, that is, a large number of the people having accepted them should abide by the norms in appropriate circumstances.

Action sociologists may be instrumental in institutionalizing the new norms of child care and development. They will motivate the people to internalize these norms as well as make them aware of the facilities given under different programmes.

VI

The strategy to be adopted by action sociologists to achieve the ends, will vary from one situation to another. They should have first-hand knowledge of the situation and of the people. However, some strategy can be outlined here. The panchayat system is in operation in rural areas. But it is well known now that it is hardly effective in rendering its services. So instead of organizing any council in which action sociologists play the key role, a few energetic young persons from the locality may be chosen and given a short orientation training in regard to the problems of child development. They should be convinced of their responsibilities. They will then look into the day-to-day problems of the children and act as a liaison between the people and the Government functionaries. Action sociologists should always be in touch with them and be their philosophers, friends and guides.

We had the occasion to experience the efficacy of the strategy. In 1979, we conducted a field study in a village in the Fatwah Block of Patna district. When we had the grasp of the problem, it was decided that some villagers should be oriented with the facilities and be motivated to work for their own people. We chose four young boys from the weaker section. All of them were matriculates. They were given training in Patna for three days. Just after a fortnight we came to know that they had approached the Block Medical Officer for immunization of the children and immunization was done. However, for want of funds, we could not maintain the link with the villagers and the selected persons got employment elsewhere. Though the effort was limited, it certainly provides necessary impetus to action sociologists.

REFERENCES

Debre, R., *Children in the Tropics*, International Children's Centre, Paris, 1979.

Government of India, *Programme of Integrated Child Care Services*, Department of Social Welfare, New delhi, 1973.

———, *National Policy for Children, op. cit.*, 1975.

———, *Health Statistics in India, op. cit.*, 1984.

Mandal, B.B. and Sinha, K.K., Rural Children — A Case Study of USFA (mimeographed). A.N. Sinha Institute of Social Studies, Patna, 1979.

Mandal, B.B., *A Study of Welfare Services of SSWA Board in Bihar.*

———, *Social Inputs in Area Development, Khagaria* (mimeographed), ANSISS, Patna, 1985.

———, *Social Inputs in Area Development, Bagaha* (mimeographed), ANSISS, Patna, 1985.

UNICEF : *An Analysis of the Situation of Children in India*, 1981.

15

ACTION SOCIOLOGY, BUREAUCRACY AND VOLUNTARY AGENCIES

NIL RATAN

Today if we have to judge by the quantity, then the Indian Social Sciences are going through a period of unprecedented progress with world congress and national conferences mushrooming, printed matter adding up, and the number of social scientists increasing at such a rate that the real purpose or task of social sciences seems to be lost. Most of the social scientists add to this flood of writing, without even considering the practical utility of their research in society. They get involved in all kinds of insignificant steps forwards or backwards on the same beaten track.

What is particularly worrying is that the flood of publications does not reveal an action-oriented social science which could be directly involved in the process of socio-economic development in India. We have a fine galaxy of illustrious social scientists but we are not utilizing them, instead, we indulge in the meaningless verbiage and useless technicalities. In comparison with a decade back, today the need for social scientists is more and their role has become even more important. Such expectations naturally call for involvement of the social scientist in the glaring social realities and instead of idolizing them the need is for combining the realm of social sciences theory with action, classrooms, teaching with applicable practical methods and to shun the elitist approach towards the existing stark depressing socio-economic realities. In fact, such a gigantic task cannot be envisaged to be complete without the involvement of white-collared bureaucracy. But social scientists and bureaucrats cannot bear the task alone since the socio-economic development of the under privileged both urban and rural areas is large, hence the responsibility should also be shouldered by voluntary agencies. The action social scientists and voluntary agencies in mutual cooperation with bureaucracy can be directly involved in the process of development.

II

Action sociology is the new re-emphasis in this development decade. Action anthropologists, applied anthropologists and field sociologists have been writing volumes about the various aspects of society more as the case study type of abstraction or in a very limited manner they have been able to apply their researches in the direct process of socio-economic development. But, this also has been a short-lived experience in most parts of India. It is, therefore, for us social scientists to find out how we can make research action relevant. Why applied anthropologists, action anthropologists and field sociologists have failed to get themselves involved in the larger process of India's socio-economic development.

Before we involve ourselves in the entangled web of finding reasons for failure of research and action we should first explain what action anthropologists, applied anthropologists and field anthropologists stand for.

Any "applied" aspect of social science deals with holistic aspects of society. It tries to meet the needs of society by planning for an all-round happiness, i.e. emphasis is on the actual functions.

The genesis of applied anthropology may be traced to the interest of anthropology in social change and problems of cultural contact consequent upon the interaction between the Western nations and the new nations of Africa and Asia. This interaction became very intense in the period following the Second World War. The anxiety of the new nations to transform their traditional societies on the lines of the West led to their interest in "planning and development". Anthropologists claimed in a general way to solve problems in which the knowledge of simple society was important. This encouraged Malinowski and others to write and study the "practical side" or what we call "applied" type of anthropology. Applied anthropology is looked upon as research specifically oriented to administrative and development problems together with the same degree of responsible participation in the process of utilizing the result of such research. The phrase "applied anthropology" in government must refer to the actual application of anthropological knowledge by those administratively responsible in the formulation and execution of government policy.

Applied anthropology may also be seen as part of a general movement of social science away from the humanistic study and towards the model of physical and biological science. The applied anthropologist can be imagined as curing the ills of society through science as the practising physician uses science to cure the body.

If modern applied anthropology is looked upon as springing from these two roots, one observes that there is at times a tendency of one or the other root to appear to be the dominant one, and even at times for these to be marked lines cleavage of incompatibility between these two aspects of anthropology in action. The first root arises out of the special interest of the anthropologist in the native people. The second affirms the possibility and urges the value of disinterested consideration of social phenomenon as a biologist might view protozoa on his microscope slide.

Now after raising some points on the applied anthropology, it would be better to highlight some major conceptions about action anthropology. The action anthropology studies the community as not only its subject but also as its object. The action anthropologist works relatively little in terms of applying knowledge. He improves and creates; he learns more from his traits than he puts into them by way of knowledge. He cannot do this practical work unless he can create new knowledge.

The action anthropologist believes that the target group knows more than him no matter how well-considered are his opinions. He has to understand deeply the "insiders' view" about certain problems. For the action anthropologist's right to self-determination has always been given priority. Persuasion, participation and not coercion or imposition are his working tools. He combines action and research. Thus the position of an action anthropologist is like that of a doctor who combines in himself the responsibility of diagnosing the disease, prescribing the medicines, following up the treatment, changing the prescription, if needed, and finally bringing health and happiness in society.

Field sociologists are those who believe that mere reliance on the texts would give only a partial view of Indian society, which at times can be biased or prejudiced in favour of one particular class, hence the need for field-work empirical tradition. A number of village studies published in the early 50s and 60s which were later followed by the other part of empirical studies remained exclusively the domain of field sociologists. Their contribution remains quite significant in broadening the theoretical issue on the approaches to the study of Indian society, in starting the field-work empirical tradition and in bringing out important concepts about socio-cultural changes taking place in village India. Their contribution is the most significant landmark in Indian sociology but from here sociologists should further involve themselves in not giving concepts only drawn from the social and economic reality but they should also think and write about the ways and means for involving themselves in the process of development in India. "There is the necessity to trigger changes in the areas where they are required most and to accelerate the pace of development in the direction highly desirable for society.

III

The role of bureaucracy in appreciating the socio-economic development of India has been typically bureaucratic, i.e. full of red-tapism, delay and apathy. Since India adopted the welfare-oriented development model with the introduction of several "from the above" type of development, there has been a long story of bungling, corruption, indifference and failures. The bureaucracy's failure to involve itself with socio-economic development not beyond brasstacks line has been its basic flaw in approaching the development problem. Development work is either taken as routine official target completion effort or put as another round of rigarmole posting. Ivory-tower approach and elitism in bureaucracy can only be removed by involving themselves with "from-the-below" type of development strategies and concepts. This would involve them in the grassroot understanding of socio-economic problems in each specific area with their each specific type of problem. It would be like reading the minds of the native people as to what do they do, how their conditions can be elevated, what measures can be taken to bring them uniformly in the mainstream of national development and how they can be made partners in the national progress like the poor rural and urban section of population, the Scheduled Castes and Scheduled Tribes, and the people living in the remote backward areas cut off from the main axis of national development.

This task cannot be complete without the active co-operation of action sociologists (or action social scientists) since they can use their years of experience, knowledge, tools, academic insight and training in understanding their specific typical problems.

They would act as social doctors to help administration at various levels in diagnosing social and economic problems and by prescribing the required appropriate strategies to facilitate the process of socio-economic transformation from backwardness to prosperity. This would herald a new administrator academician development approach at national level to induce social and economic development among the rural, urban and tribal populations of India. Some States have tried and left it and some are in the process of trying. This should be taken up uniformly by involving action sociologists and administrators together in the gigantic task of development. The uniqueness of development and its futuristic impact and consequences can only be understood by the uniqueness of academic mind and training.

IV

In India after Independence, the voluntary agencies have been involved more and more to take up development of the under-privileged. This is a consequence of a feeling among the planners that in a developing Welfare State the responsibility for socio-economic development is not only to be carried by the State but it should be shouldered also in the wider areas by the voluntary agencies. Today, voluntary agencies, are looked upon as engines of social change and social development. They can perform many difficult tasks efficiently and with minimum resources.

Any voluntary agency which is involved in the task of development will have to face difficulties either in terms of men or material. They have to foresee all this in order to take up any challenging task. In order to achieve their objective, they would have to mobilize public opinion, involve the Government, and other voluntary agencies in discussing the problems of development and how to plan a strategy to achieve the necessary objective. They would have to build confidence in the minds of planners, bureaucrats, public men about their sincerity, devotion and dedication. In the voluntary agencies approach to development, there is no other path except that of sacrifice, dedication, duty and devotion, for the betterment of society. We should learn by the experience of voluntary agencies like the Sulabh International, Patna.

There are problems of poor men, women, bonded labour, Scheduled Caste and Scheduled Tribe children, insanitation, rehabilitation of night-soil carriers, destitute children who are homeless and unwanted. But importantly the whole grey area of human existence is utterly unimportant for most of the citizen. People have a vague notion that someone takes care of these problems. There are such "Someones" but they are too few and those which exist are riddled with resource, manpower and other problems. The voluntary agencies have to raise consciousness of the public opinion also, to do much more in these areas. The voluntary agencies will have to take help and cooperation of action sociologists in identifying such social problems and to devise ways and means with the help of bureaucracy and action sociologists to solve such problems. The voluntary agencies, action social scientists, public and bureaucracy have to shoulder together this giant task of accelerating the process of development.

To conclude, one can make a fervent appeal to all those who are concerned with this task of development that they have to acknowledge and take help of action sociologists along with voluntary agencies and public themselves for the implementation of action research and action programmes in India.

Gandhiji's basic teaching was for a comprehensive system aimed not only at educating the mind and to achieve socio-economic independence but also to help them build up character and dignity of attitude in order to merge with all types of streams in order to be called the national mainstream.

IV

SOCIAL DIMENSIONS OF LOW COST SANITATION

16

THE SULABH MOVEMENT

BINDESHWAR PATHAK

Sulabh Shauchalaya represents widely accepted low-cost option to solve the problems of disposal of human excreta in a scientific manner. It has an innovative technological design appropriate to the felt need of the people. It is in conformity with the needs and aspirations of the people. Its compatibility with the aspirations of the people has led to its large-scale adoption in the country. Its large-scale acceptance among the people has been possible through adequate understanding of the attitudinal orientation of the people and subjecting the same to effective social intervention. Environmental or social system constraints were diagnosed before the launching of this programme among the people.

Adoption is a highly intertwined and dependent process. In between diffusion and acceptance, a number of intervening variables exist. Many of them are sociological in nature. Any attempt at ensuring widespread adoption of any technological innovation has to take into account the sociological variables. In fact it may be noted that prior to the arrival of the Sulabh Shauchalaya on the national scene a number of low-cost alternatives to sewerage and septic tank existed. These, however, remained potential technology. Those who designed these schemes had betrayed complete ignorance of the social realities. As such these technologies could not find place in society. Also as an action sociologist engineer the failures on the part of the predecessors of low-cost designs were apprehended by me in advance. In fact, the experience of these experiments led me to modify the technology to cater to the needs of the people and to identify the difficult areas for social intervention to ensure wider acceptance of this scheme. Thus, in the beginning I had to confront opposition from the people to get septic latrines constructed in their houses. In fact while adhering to my conviction about the effectiveness of Sulabh Shauchalaya in solving the problems, I had to understand the human psychology in order to change the same. I provided alternatives to the people as per their wishes. These, however, appeared to them more expensive than the scheme which I was propagating. As a result people's wrong notions about certain expensive and socially undesirable solutions to the problem of disposal of human excreta crumbled.

Our initiatives today have acquired dimensions of a movement which now represents collective mobilization for bringing about a change in the attitude and behaviour of the people. The Sulabh ideology is wedded to the abolition of the practice of carrying night-soil as headloads. People have favoured this scheme on account of the initiatives made by us. These initiatives are based on social realities. The continuation of traditional exploitative method of disposal of human excreta is not regarded desirable any longer. In fact, the past arrangements which are socially incompatible do not find favour among the people any longer. Thus, it was through the emphasis on the social diamensions of Sulabh Shauchalaya that the low-cost technological option has acquired the status of an effective technology. Earlier experiments ended as exercises in potential technology in the absence of the insight needed for social engineering. The people have now perceived it to be the best possible alternative that they can afford. In their opinion also it is not technologically inferior to the existing technological options. In fact it has marked an improvement on the existing outdated and exploitative method of excreta disposal.

The achievements are the result of the technological modifications as well as social engineering that underly the Sulabh philosophy. Sulabh Shauchalaya is not only a technological innovation, it has a technology with human face. Prior to the spread of this scheme among the people there was emphasis on expensive and socially incompatible designs. As a result there were a few takers of the ingredients of modern sanitation culture. The majority of the people tended to remain deprived. They did not either have any arrangement to solve their basic problems of disposal of human excreta so they had to resort to method that was socially disastrous and medically harmful. As a social engineer it was my conviction that until and unless the importance of providing these facilities to people was taken note of, we were likely to create a situation of discrimination and deprivation. In this way, the very ideology for the spread of Sulabh Shauchalaya is oriented to the emerging egalitarian conceptualization of development in the developing countries. This is an important ingredient in the programmes of Sulabh Shauchalaya. Thus, through the scheme of community toilets, the movement aims at covering the left and the unnoticed. It has also helped people mobilize to run a scheme for their welfare with their cooperation.

The Sulabh experiment has also brought about a change of an unprecedented magnitude. It has led to the elimination of the practice of carrying night-soil by a specific caste of the Indian society. These people are looked down upon for their association with the job of disposal of night-soil. Since Independence a number of steps have been taken to ameliorate the condition of the untouchables. These, however, failed to solve the problem of the lowest in the hierarchy of the Scheduled Caste responsible for the disposal of human excreta. It was through the implementation of the Sulabh schemes of excreta disposal that the problem of scavenging was attended to for the first time in the most effective manner. Today a number of towns have been declared scavenging-free on account of the successful implementation of the Sulabh programmes.

It is, therefore, clear that the spread of technology has been possible after obtaining an understanding of the socio-psychological barriers to the adoption of these schemes. In fact strategies based on an understanding of the reality have led to the widespread acceptance of this scheme by the people. The important success of a scheme of national importance has been possible through the techniques of social engineering. It has also been successful on account of the visible social impact that followed the implementation of this scheme of latrine construction. Technology alone is not sufficient. Its social ingredients together with the sociological skills to spread it among the people are equally important. Engineering helps creation of infrastructure. However, in order to be embedded in society the technological innovations have to be socially relevant. These are also required to be skilfully transmitted among the people.

17

REHABILITATION OF LIBERATED SCAVENGERS

B.N. SRIVASTAVA

India is the only country in the world where only a particular section of society is traditionally responsible for keeping the habitation clean by removing the waste products of the society including the human excreta. This is a disgrace to the country. Instances are not rare even today when one can see people carrying night soil in buckets on their heads or removing human excreta by physical touch. Who are these people? Why they are compelled to do such type of inhuman and dirty work and how long these neglected sections of society will remain under such bondage? Is there any solution to liberate them before we enter of the 21st century? These are some of the complex questions which are agitating the minds of the well-meaning people in the country. The country which won freedom from the slavery of the British people 41 years ago is not able to liberate from human bondage more than one million people who are called Bhangis, Mehtars, Balmikis, etc., and are still engaged in their traditional occupation of sweeping and scavenging. Is it not a shame on us when we force a person to clean excreta of others?

What is Scavenging

Scavenging covers a variety of activities such as cleaning of roads, water-borne latrines, carrying of refuse and cleaning of dry-latrines. It is the cleaning of dry latrines by primitive methods and carrying of night soil which represent the most obnoxious aspect of scavenging. This so-called "unclean" occupation has traditionally been closely linked to the practice of untouchability.

Extent of Problem

It has been estimated that only 0.5 per cent of the rural population in India has access to sanitary facilities for the disposal of human waste. Almost the entire rural population (estimated at about 522 million people, according to the 1981 Census) defecate in the open.

In a UNDP-assisted survey of 210 towns in 11 States and 3 Union Territories, it was found that 27 per cent of the people of these towns had flush latrines; about 40 per cent dry-latrines (12.78 million households) and a staggering 33 per cent (10.43 million urban houses) had no latrines whatsoever.

Sewerage System

The waste products including the human excreta is collected, carried and disposed of manually to a safe point of disposal by the sweepers and scavengers. This primitive method of collecting and disposing of society's waste has now been modernized to some extent and replaced by a system in which these wastes are mixed with sufficient quantity of water and carried through closed conduits under the condition of gravity flow. This mixture of water and waste products, popularly called sewage, thus automatically flows up to the place from where it is disposed of after giving it suitable treatment, thus avoiding the carriage of waste on heads or carts. The treated sewage effluents may be disposed of either in a running body of water, such as stream, or may be used for irrigating crops.

This modern water-carried sewage has completely replaced the old conservancy system of sanitation in the developed countries like the USA. However, being a developing country, India still uses the old conservancy system at various places, particularly in small towns. The metropolitan cities and bigger towns of our country, no doubt, have already been equipped with the facilities of this modern water sewerage system; and attempts are being made to equip the remaining towns and cities with this system, but this depends upon the availability of resources. In the developing countries modern sewerage system is preferred to the old conservancy system as it is more hygienic because in this system society's wastes have not to be collected and carried in buckets or carts as is required to be done in the conservancy system. The free carriage of night-soil in trucks or as head load which is required in the conservancy system may pose health hazards to sweepers/scavengers and other residents because of the possibilities of flies and insects transmitting disease germs from these accessible carts to the residents' food and eatables; whereas in the modern sewerage system no such danger exists because the polluted sewage is carried in closed conduits as soon as it is produced.

Inadequacy of Resources

In spite of these advantages it has not been possible to completely replace the old conservancy system mainly because huge capital funds are required for the construction of such a system. Moreover, for the functioning of a sewerage system, ample amount of water must be available to the people and hence reliable and assured water supply must, first, be installed before installing a sewerage system.

Water-Seal Latrines

The household bucket privy system exists as a crude, ugly and avoidable reality in India. A search has to be on for an economical, safe and hygienic system, other than the sewerage and septic tank for the disposal of human excreta which can be adopted on a mass scale. Various international agencies, notably WHO, UNICEF and UNDP have been engaged in evaluating the methods for removal of any possible defects in order to ensure their mass adoption. In India the hand-flush water-seal sanitary latrines developed by PRAI, UNDP and Sulabh have become popular. The design generally consists of plinth, pan, water-seal, drain, tanks and tank cover. The pan and water-seal are connected with two leaching pits, of which one functions at a time while the other is kept closed. The second pit is opened for use when the first is filled up. While the second pit is in use, the human excreta gets transformed into manure in the first tank. The main advantages in constructing such type of latrine is that it is odourless as the gases produced are absorbed in the soil. There is no danger of air pollution as the water seal does not allow the gases to go out of the pit and as such, no gas-pipe is needed for the system. Similarly, there is no possibility of any bacteria to break the water seal and come out on the surface to pollute any nearby after source. It is easy to construct such type of latrines which are quite economical. The space required for them is also small and can be provided even in the corridor, verandah or bedroom of the house. There is no danger to the foundation of the walls or other structures in the house. Another advantage is that it can be constructed in different soil conditions and under varying depths of subsoil watertable. A small quantity of water is required to flush out the human waste from the pan to the leaching pits. The design evolved by the Sulabh International is definitely an improvement over others.

A number of designs of alternative water borne/other latrines have been prepared by different agencies in the country. It will be necessary to pool all such designs suitable to different parts of the country and give them wide publicity and circulation. A programme of dry latrines' conversion within a period of five years will require sizeable financial resources.

Malkani Committee

In 1957 the Ministry of Home Affairs appointed a committee under the chairmanship of Prof. N. R. Malkani to prepare a scheme to put an end to the degrading practice of scavengers having to carry night-soil in buckets or baskets. The committee submitted its report in 1960 and recommended several measures for improving the working and living conditions of scavengers. The committee observed that the best system for the disposal of night soil through mechanized means is flush-out latrines, but heavy investment is required if all the towns and cities are connected with a sewerage system. The committee, therefore, recommended improved methods of scavenging such as use of wheel barrows, gum boots, gloves and other modern equipments.

Schemes of the Government of India

Based on the recommendations of the Malkani Committee, the Ministry of Home Affairs introduced a Centrally-sponsored scheme for giving grant-in-aid to the municipalities for the purchase of wheel-barrows, gum-boots, gloves and other equipments in the Third Five Year Plan. Another Centrally-sponsored scheme was introduced during the same Plan providing houses and house sites to the scavengers and sweepers in the municipalities. But both the schemes could not make much headway due to certain inherent limitations and, therefore, dropped during the Fourth Five Year Plan.

Measures for Eradicating Scavenging

While discussing the problem of scavenging our late Prime Minister,

Smt. Indira Gandhi, once said in Parliament: "Everybody is conscious of this fact, and we have discussed it many times and there is no doubt that this is a disgrace and it should be eradicated as early as possible. . ." "You cannot ban a thing unless you provide an alternative thing for them. These people will be out of job, this is the problem. I have no objection to doing it myself and I might tell him that in Gandhi Ashram I have cleaned that thing." It will be necessary to adopt the following twin approach in dealing with the problem of scavenging. Firstly, it is necessary to abolish the practice of scavenging through appropriate legislation. Secondly, suitable alternative means of human waste disposal through conversion of existing dry latrines into sanitary ones will have to be made. These measures also presuppose that the existing scavenging population will be suitably rehabilitated in alternative economic occupations without diminution of the present income of the family. The legislation should ban the construction of houses with dry latrines and no new construction should be allowed without provision of appropriate arrangements for human waste disposal. The legislation should also empower the municipalities/ Government authorities to convert dry latrines wherever the house-owners fails to do so and recover the cost of conversion from them.

Progress of Work Done So Far

A beginning was made during the Fifth Five-year Plan by the Union Ministry of Works and Housing (now Ministry of Urban Development). A Centrally-sponsored scheme for the conversion of dry-laterines into water-borne latrines was taken up with a small provision of Rs. 4.40 crores. The scheme, however, could not make headway and was, therefore, dropped.

Centrally-sponsored Scheme of Ministry of Welfare

During the Sixth Five-year Plan, the Ministry of Home Affairs (subject now transferred to the Ministry of Welfare) introduced a special scheme to liberate these scavengers from their demeaning occupation in a number of States on matching grant basis. Concurrently with the conversion of dry-latrines into water-seal latrines, the Government had also taken up simultaneously a programme to rehabilitate these scavengers by re-training them for other more productive and dignified occupations. In Bihar they were trained as electricians, motor mechanics, motor drivers, carpenters, masons etc. In other States they were trained in different trades, and are now gainfully employed in dignified occupations. After training they were rehabilitated under self-employment programmes. In Uttar Pradesh, they were allotted shops and given financial assistance for starting various trades and business. This scheme was further intensified during the Seventh Five Year Plan. So far 166 towns have been taken up for the conversion of dry-latrines into water-borne ones on the whole-town approach basis, out of which 32 towns have been declared scavenging-free up to March 1988. The number of scavengers rehabilitated in these 166 towns was about 10,000 out of a total 27,000 scavengers. The number of dry-latrines converted into water-borne latrines was 2.73 lakh out of a total of 6.55 lakh existing in these towns.

Ministry of Urban Development and State Governments

In addition to the above-mentioned special programme taken up by the Ministry of Welfare, the Ministry of Urban Development also provides financial assistance (loan) to the State Governments under an IDSMT programme for low-cost sanitation on a small scale, similarly, some of the State Governments have also taken up this programme under their State Plans with financial assistance (loan) from HUDCO.

It is thus evident that looking at the magnitude of the problem, very little work has been done so far and at this rate India cannot hope to be scavenging free even by 2000 A.D.

Progress of Rehabilitation

It is true that the progress of both the schemes of conversion of dry-latrines into pour-flush latrines as well as the rehabilitation of displaced scavengers are rather slow. In a number of States the work relating to the conversion of dry-latrines was undertaken in isolation without taking up any programme for the rehabilitation of scavengers. Even in States where the rehabilitation programme has been taken up, its progress is very slow. Though the Government of India in the Ministry of Welfare provides Special Central Assistance to the State Governments for programmes of economic development for enabling the Scheduled Caste families to cross over the poverty line, this money is not being used for the training and rehabilitation of scavengers to the extent necessary. According to the Ministry's guidelines the work relating to the conversion is to be done simultaneously. Up to a maximum of 10 per cent of the SCA is earmarked for the economic development of vulnerable groups such as scavengers, sweepers, denotified, nomadic and semi-nomadic communities and bonded labourers. Considerable flexibility has been given to the States in the utilization of SCA so that suitable schemes can be taken up for the rehabilitation of displaced scavengers and their dependents according to the local conditions, which vary from place to place. While some State Governments such as Andhra Pradesh, Bihar, Uttar Pradesh, etc., have taken up schemes for the rehabilitation of scavengers in right earnest, other States are lagging behind in this respect. The Government of Maharashtra is also going to set up a centre in Thane district soon for providing necessary training to the displaced scavengers.

The programme of conversion of dry-laterines into pour-flush latrines in a town is preceded by a detailed preliminary survey with a view to knowing the number of scavengers engaged, their age-group, marital status, educational qualification, aptitude for other occupations, etc. This information helps the State government in undertaking suitable training and rehabilitation programmes for the scavengers and their dependents. While municipal scavengers are absorbed in the municipality itself, the problem remains in the case of private scavengers and their dependents. The Ministry of Welfare provides financial assistance to the Stage Governments (mostly Departments of Urban Development or Local Self-Government) for the conversion of dry-latrines under the Centrally-sponsored Scheme of "Liberation of Scavengers" whereas the expenditure on the training and rehabilitation of scavengers is to be met out of Special Central Assistance which is released to the Department dealing with the welfare of Scheduled Castes/Scheduled Tribes at the State level.

Coordination Committee

The Government of India has been stressing the need to set up Coordination Committees at the State level consisting of the representatives of the Departments of Urban Developments, Welfare (dealing with Scheduled Castes/Scheduled Tribes) and Scheduled Caste Development Corporation, to sort out the various problems concerning the training and rehabilitation of displaced scavengers.

Such committees have been set up in a number of States but they are not effective. They do not meet frequently. These committees have to be made effective so that the work of conversion of dry-laterines and rehabilitation of displaced scavengers could be done simultaneously.

Time-Lag Between Training and Rehabilitation

In some States it has been noticed that although the displaced scavengers and their dependents were provided training in various trades, their actual rehabilitation took sufficient time and there was a wide time gap in their training and actual rehabilitation. This gap sometimes defeats the very purpose of the training and the trainee forgets whatever he has learnt. Efforts should, therefore, be made to reduce this gap.

Role of Scheduled Castes Development Corporations

The Scheduled Castes Development Corporations can play a very important role in providing necessary training and rehabilitating the displaced persons. The training can be organized by them through the existing institutions like ITI, etc., or special institutions can be set up for this purpose as has been done by some of the State governments where the existing facilities were not adequate. The training could be imparted to those who are in the age group up to 35 or 40 years. Others can be rehabilitated straightway in alternative employment. There may be special training programmes for women.

For rehabilitating displaced persons suitable workable schemes will have to be formulated with the component of bank loans, margin money loan or subsidy as the case may be. The self-employment schemes may vary from trade to trade. For instance, if someone is trained as a motor mechanic or electrician, blacksmith, tailor, etc., he can be given financial assistance through bank loan, margin money loan, etc., for buying necessary tools and equipment. Similarly if somebody has been trained as leather workers, backward and forward linkage may be established with the leather corporations, tannery, etc., so that the trained person could be provided financial assistance for purchase of raw material and marketing of finished goods. This will apply to similar other trades as well like carpet-making, *duree*-making, etc. The displaced persons can be allotted shops in the main market by the municipalities where these persons can start business with financial help from the Government. The persons who have been trained in tailoring, garment-making, carpentry, etc., can be given work by various departments of the Government like supply of uniforms, furniture etc. The Scheduled Caste Development Corporation, U.P. has set up 21 short-hand and typing training centres for the Scheduled Caste. Such centres can be set up by other State governments also. Special rehabilitation programmes will have to be chalked out for women and children who are mostly engaged in scavenging.

The municipalities can allot house sites, shops, etc., to the displaced scavengers. The municipal scavengers may be provided with suitable accommodation and educational facilities for their children. The State governments will have to involve banks in a big way for providing credit facilities at a low rate of interest. The Scheduled Castes Development Corporations can take guarantee on behalf of the beneficiaries for the refund of bank loans.

Monitoring and Evaluation

There is lack of proper monitoring of the progress of conversion schemes as well as the rehabilitation of displaced scavengers. This results in a big gap and a number of displaced families remain uncovered. There is, therefore, need for an effective monitoring both at the municipality and State levels.

None of the State Governments have conducted any evaluative studies with a view to assessing the impact of these programmes and find out shortcomings and bottlenecks, if any, at the implementation stage. The Planning Commission has entrusted such a study to Social Services Research Institute in Delhi. The study has been undertaken in three towns of Bihar and one town in Rajasthan. The report is awaited. It is desirable that such studies should be undertaken by all the concerned State Governments.

Other Programmes for the Welfare of Scavengers

In the caste hierarchy among the Scheduled Castes, the scavengers have been given the lowest position in view of their unclean occupation. They derive benefit from the various schemes undertaken for the development of the Scheduled Castes, viz., Special Component Plans, Special Central Assistance, Scheduled Caste Development Corporations, Centrally-sponsored Schemes etc. The State governments have been asked to formulae special schemes for the social, educational and economic development of the scavengers, sweepers, etc. As said earlier, the State governments have been authorized to utilize up to a maximum of 10 per cent of the Special Central Assistance for the economic development of vulnerable groups including scavengers, sweepers, etc. Some of the State governments have formulated special schemes for their socio-economic development.

"Pre-Matric Scholarships for the Children of those engaged in Unclean Occupations"

The Ministry of Welfare has introduced a Centrally-sponsored Scheme of Pre-matric scholarships of the children of those engaged in unclean occupations viz., scavengers, flayers, tanners and sweepers who have traditional links with the profession of scavenging. The main objective of the scheme is to provide good quality of education to the children from these groups by keeping them away from the unhygienic surrounding under which their parents live. They are kept in hostels and the entire expenditure on their education is met by the Government. The children studying in Classes VI to X are covered under this scheme. They are paid scholarships at the rate of Rs. 200 p.m. per student in Classes VI to VII and Rs. 250 p.m. per student for those studying Classes IX and X subject to the economic limit of Rs. 1,000 p.m. for parents. All children from these groups irrespective of religion are covered under the scheme. It is proposed to modify this scheme suitably by extending the coverage of this scheme to Classes III to X instead of Classes VI to X as at present inclusion of day scholars, and upward revision of parents' income limit.

Conclusion

It will not be denied by anyone that the existence of the practice of scavenging is a shame to the country. It also has obvious relevance to the untouchability situation. A time-bound programme must, therefore, figure in the Plan so that by the end of four or five years there is no scavenging in this country and the present "scavengers" are suitably accommodated in other occupations. This is a task within the range of possibility, technology is available. There are different alternative types of low-cost sanitation for which a sewerage system is not the *sine qua non.* While the Ministry of Welfare or Urban Development would be in the best position to work out a total scheme for this purpose, it appears broadly that this can be achieved by a provision of about Rs. 2,000 crores. This would appear to be capable of covering not only conversion of existing latrines in all classes of towns but also provide new water-sealed closets where no latrines exist, and thus fulfil the dream of Mahatma Gandhi.

18

LOW COST SANITATION IN TAMIL NADU : Social Aspects

PAUL P. APPASAMY and D. SUNDARAM

"Sanitation" has never been a major investment priority in India although it is well known that protected water supply and sanitary waste disposal are vital for the health and well-being of any community. The impetus for improvements in sanitation has primarily been due to the United Nations designating the current decades as the International Drinking Water Supply and Sanitation Decade. The Government of India started the National Water Supply and Sanitation Decade (NWSSD) programme from April 1, 1981. The Ministry of Works and Housing has advised the State Governments to provide funds in the Sixth Plan (1980-85) and Seventh Plan (1985-90) periods to achieve the Decade targets. Subsequently these targets have been scaled down, since adequate resources are not available to meet the targets by March 31, 1991.

In 1985, roughly half the population had no sanitation facilities at all, a quarter had dry latrines (mainly in the rural areas and small towns), and rest (about 23%) had sewerage or septic tank systems. Despite the pleas of leaders like Mahatma Gandhi that sanitation be accorded high priority, successive governments at both national and State levels ignored this *basic need* for more than three decades. Urban areas, particularly the metropolitan areas, were able to demand and obtain expensive water-borne sewerage systems. Although there have been problems with ultimate treatment and disposal which have caused water pollution (for example, the Yamuna in Delhi and the Cooum in Madras), urban households, tiny and large, have benefited in terms of access to municipal sewerage systems.

The high cost of sewerage systems has inevitably meant that scanty or no facilities are provided for the poor. Neglect is greatest in urban slums, in urban fringe areas, in small towns and in most villages. In rural areas, the paucity of funds is compounded by inadequate *institutions* for operation and maintenance. We will return to this crucial point later in the paper. Thus improvements in sanitation services can be caused only by:

(a) a much higher level of financing than has been the case,
(b) by creating the appropriate institutional structures especially in non-metropolitan areas; and
(c) by choosing appropriate technologies that are less expensive and easier to operate.

The rationale for including sanitation as a *investment* in plan allocation is not merely for improving civic services (or amenities). Rather, the purpose of waste disposal is to limit the spreading of diseases, particularly water-borne diseases. Thus, sanitation must be viewed as a public health measure, which causes an *improvement in the health status of the community.* A study on cholera prevention in the Philippines concluded that "Sanitation proves both to be more effective and less expensive than vaccination, especially in long-term programmes for control and elimination of cholera from endemic areas". Thus, investment in sanitation is economically justifiable as a means of preventing the spread of many diseases that are widely prevalent in urban and rural areas of India. *"Disease prevention"* decreases the cost of treatment, improves productivity, and more generally improves health status by reducing the levels of morbidity and mortality. The link between sanitation and health is an important one for politicians/government officials on the one hand, and the general public on the other to understand. For the former, such understanding is important in the formulation and implementation of public policy and programmes; for the latter, it is crucial in terms of acceptance. "Given the paucity of resources, costs have to be incurred by the public, even the poor, if a strategy for sanitation is to succeed. This cost may be the 30 paise paid by a slum dweller at a pay-and-use toilet, or, it may be the monthly sewerage bill that the urban consumer pays. While the Government can/should subsidize the capital cost of any sanitation system, it must have the means of recovering at least part of the cost of operation and maintenance. If such a partnership can be built between the public agencies and the public, a beginning can be made in dealing with the problem of sanitation. However, the first step is to recognize that water supply and sanitation are priority areas for *development.* The choice of technologies, the implementation of programmes and the acceptance of these programmes by the pubic are issues that have to be dealt with carefully. Thus, the designation of the National Water Supply and Sanitation Decade by the Government of India was of more than symbolic importance. It was a clear signal to government departments and to the public, that there was a commitment at the highest levels providing these basic needs. The concomitant allocation of resources provided the means, albeit limited, to reach these goals by March, 31, 1991. In the following paragraphs, we will discuss the magnitude of the problem in Tamil Nadu, and the sanitation goals established by the State government. We will then move on to a discussion of the socio-economic and institutional aspects in implementing sanitation programmes, and conclude with some policy recommendations.

Sanitation in Tamil Nadu

The 1981 Census enumerates the total population of the State of Tamil Nadu to be 48 million, with one-third (16 million) living in 434 urban areas. These urban areas consist of three corporations (Madras, Coimbatore and Madurai), 123 municipalities and townships, and the rest in town panchayats. Of these, only the three major corporations, 12 municipalities and two townships have underground sewerage systems (Table 18.1). Excluding Madras City, the total population covered is less than three million or roughly 20 per cent of the total urban population. If we include Madras City, 48 per cent of the urban population has sanitation services. The remaining 52 per cent have to cope with inadequate sanitation measures.

Under the NWSSD programme, it has been decided that safe and sanitary methods of waste disposal will be provided to 80 per cent of the urban population. The following targets have been set for March 1991:

(a) Sewerage systems for 100 per cent of Class I cities,
(b) Safe and sanitary waste disposal for 50 per cent of Class II and other cities.

The breakdown of the urban population by size-class is shown in Table 18.2. The rural population of 24 million is distributed across the State in 15,831 villages.

TABLE 18.1: Urban Areas with Underground Sewerage

CLASS I CITIES (9)		CLASS II CITIES (3)	
Madras	(C)	Chidambaram	(M)
Coimbatore	(C)	Ootacamund	(M)
Madurai	(C)	Mannargudi (partial)	(M)
Tiruchirapalli	(M)		
Kancheepuram	(M)	CLASS III CITIES (4)	
Thiruvothiyur	(M)		
Thirunelveli	(M)	Thirumangalam (partial)	(M)
Tuticorin	(M)	Sathur	(M)
Kumbakonam	(M)	Mettur	(T)
		Periakulam	(M)
		CLASS IV CITY (1)	
		Aravangadu (T)	

C—Corporation M—Municipality T—Township

Source: Nagarajan (1987).

TABLE 18.2: Population by Size Class of Urban Tamil Nadu

Class	Size	No. of cities	Population (in million)	Percentage
I	> 100,000	21	7.832*	62.22
II	50,000 – 99,999	41	2.747	15.97
III	20,000 – 49,999	89	2.758	12.51
IV	10,000 – 19,999	123	1.765	7.39
V	5,000 – 9,999	90	0.645	1.77
VI	< 9,999	70	0.205	0.14
Total		434	15.952	100.00

* Population of Madras City 3.276 million and that of Madurai and Coimbatore 1.525 million. The remaining 18 Class I cities account for only 3.031 million.

Source: Census of India (1981) — General Population Tables, Tamil Nadu.

By comparing Tables 18.1 and 18.2 we note the following:

1. Other than Madras, Coimbatore and Madurai, only 6 of the 18

Class I cities have underground sewerage, i.e. the remaining 12 cities have to be sewered if the 1991 target is to be met.

2. In size Classes II and III only 7 out of 130 have sewerage. Providing safe waste disposal (even if it is not sewerage) has to be extended to 50 per cent of these towns.
3. Size Classes IV, V and VI consisting of 283 towns have no sewerage with the exception of Aravangadu). Safe water disposal has to be provided to at least 50 per cent of these towns.

The magnitude of the 1991 targets is indeed substantial. The resources allocated under the NWSSD Programmes of Tamil Nadu for Water Supply and Sanitation were Rs. 1,206 crores (1980 prices). There is little doubt that the resources available severely limit the areas where underground sewerage can be provided. In fact, even the major Class I cities cannot provide sewerage to their entire population. Fringe areas and slums areas are often left unsewered. For example, in Madras City, of the 12 panchayats added to the city in 1978, there are plans for providing sewerage to only three (Villivakkam, Tiruvanmiyur and Saligramam). There are more than a thousand slums in Madras but only few of these have access to sanitation services (TNSCB, 1972). Similar situations prevail in other Class I cities. Thus, there is a need for introducing low-cost sanitation services not only in the smaller towns, but also in the fringe areas and slum areas of the Class I cities. The task of providing sanitation services in the 15,000 villages of the State can only be described as a mammoth undertaking. The resources allocated for rural areas are like the proverbial drop in the ocean.

Socio-Economic Aspects

Successful implementation of a sanitation programme requires consideration of the following aspects:

(a) Choice of Technology
(b) Diffusion of the Technology (by institutions)
(c) Adoption and acceptance of the Technology (by users).

We will discuss each of these aspects briefly.

Technology Choice: Low-cost sanitation measures range from the pit latrines to septic tanks. Bhargava *et al.*, suggest the following typology in categorizing sanitation technologies in India. The most basic types include dry latrines such as pit privies, bored hole latrines, bucket latrines and compost latrines. Some of these like bucket latrines require the use of scavengers for removal of the waste. Public opinion in recent years has characterized scavenging as a *dehumanizing* occupation. It has been suggested that alternative occupations be provided to scavengers. The *Sulabh Shauchalaya* movement was launched to provide a viable alternative to the appalling practice of using human beings to collect and transport human wastes. However, some of the other dry technologies like the modified pit privies and composting may be viable alternatives to open defecation, particularly in villages and small towns where there is a serious lack of water. Since, Tamil Nadu has many areas where water is a scarce commodity, these technologies could be employed. After decomposition, the manure could be used as fertilizer for non-food crops or for trees.

The second category involving the use of water, includes technologies such as pour flush toilets, aquaprivies, septic tanks, etc. These technologies cannot be used where the soil is not suitable for soakaways or where the housing density or water-table is too high. In particular septic tanks (which are popular in unsewered urban areas) require sufficient water for flushing, and sufficient land with permeable soil for effluent disposal.

The third category includes new technologies or new designs of earlier technologies. New technologies include chemical toilets and vacuum toilets, which are considered to be too expensive in the Indian context. New designs include the "Sulabh Shauchalaya" which is a water-based composting latrine, and a similar modification by the Central Building Research Institute. The major advantage of these designs is that the composting reduces the wastes to an organic manure which is both easier to remove and has good fertilizer value, eliminating the need for scavengers.

In Tamil Nadu, the Institute of Public Health, Poonamallee, has undertaken a research-cum-action project (RCAP) in low-cost sanitation. The RCAP has developed a low-cost, hand-flushed, water seal, leach pit, sanitary latrine. The RCAP latrine has been employed in both urban and rural areas. However, as is the case with any water-based sanitation system, the soil has to be suitable for the leach pit to function properly; also, close proximity of toilets or high water table has been observed to cause problems in implementation in the slum areas of Madras City.

It is not our intention to discuss the specific technologies of low-cost sanitation, or their pros and cons in this section. Those interested could consult some of the references, or any standard manual on low-cost sanitation. Rather, our purpose is to reflect on those factors that govern the choice of technology. The most obvious (but often overlooked) factor is that of *technological feasibility*. This does not refer to feasibility in laboratory or controlled conditions. Feasibility refers to the particular environment where the technology will be employed. There is no point in recommending a water-based system where there is an acute water shortage. People may consider it a waste to transport water from a long distance for the purpose of flushing. Similarly, soil conditions, housing density, the depth of the water-table and many other environmental factors govern the use of the technology.

Next, the technology must be *cost efficient*, and be *affordable* to the user. We have already referred to the dire lack of resources. It would be impossible for the Government to undertake the full cost of sanitation, particularly for operation and maintenance. The latter costs which can be considerable are often overlooked by government agencies, in their anxiety to meet targets for the number of latrines or public conveniences built. In the case of individual toilets, it is often the case that the household is willing to bear part of the capital cost, and will assume the responsibility for maintenance. Periodic cleaning of the leach pit or septic tank can be done by the agency. In the case of public conveniences, the "pay-and-use" system has been much more successful than the free system in almost every case. The payment by the user is adequate to cover the operating cost of the public conveniences. Thus, the selection of the technology must be done with care, giving due consideration to capital and recurrent costs, and the possibility of cost-sharing by the user.

A third factor in the choice of technology is that it must be *understandable* to the user. Pour flush toilets, for example, can get choked up if other solid wastes are thrown into the toilet. Some technologies require a minimum quantity of water for flushing. In the double leach pit system, it is necessary to close one pit after it fills up, and connect the other pit, and so on. The need to educate the user in the maintenance of the system may be crucial. In other words, a technology that the user has difficulty in understanding, is an *inappropriate* one. This simple fact is often overlooked by engineers and planners who are excited about new designs and new technologies. It is tragic that even well-educated, high-income individuals who travel on international flights invariably misuse or choke up the chemical or vacuum toilets found in aeroplanes. It should, therefore, not be surprising that poorer people living in urban slums or in rural areas have difficulties in understanding a technology that they have previously not encountered.

Lastly, the technology must *fulfil the user needs and expectations.* In other words, the user must be sufficiently aware of the technology that he *demands.* This may result from a demonstration project or from a neighbour or friend having the amenity. However, it is counter-productive to provide a service that is not wanted. The classic case in Madras City was the water closet provided by the Slum Clearance Board in their tenements. In some instances, the water closet was covered up and the room converted for some other purpose which the resident deemed to be more useful. (Lack of water in the upper stories compounded the problem.) When the user *demands* the technology and is willing to maintain it, then the technology has a greater chance of success. In short, there is no point in supplying a technology for which there is no demand.

The next set of factors in implementation relates to *diffusion of technology.* These concern the establishment of an institutional framework and programmes to deliver the service. These factors include:

(i) responsiveness,
(ii) health education,
(iii) training/instruction,
(iv) delegation authority,
(v) efficient delivery and
(vi) monitoring/evaluation.

We will discuss some of these aspects in the next section on institutional aspects.

The most crucial aspect of implementation is *adoption and acceptance* by the community. Most bureaucratic organizations view their role as "service providers" and the community as passive recipients. There is little recognition that no programme for sanitation, housing, irrigation or whatsoever can be successfully implemented without the input and participation of the recipients. While a lot of lip-service has been paid to community participation, in reality most agencies neither have the experts nor the willingness to take this task seriously. The extent to which most agencies are willing to go in this direction is to inform the local leadership (in a village or town or slum). If the leaders agree, the project is implemented by the technical personnel of the agency, often with the help of contractors and labourers drawn from outside the area. When the project is implemented, the executing agency leaves the area with some minimal instruction to the local people. This mode of operation (implementation) often called the "engineering approach", is clearly undesirable in the case of services such as sanitation which affect the life-style of almost every individual in the community.

Communities must have input to design, scheduling, training, financing and enforcement. It must be an equal partner with the agency. They must be willing participants in the experiment where they contribute time, finance, and local expertise, which complements the resources and expertise of the agency. Otherwise, there will be no commitment to maintenance, to paying operating costs and ultimately to the continuity of the project. It is beyond the scope of this paper to examine why the "top-down" approach is used. Many have speculated that the feudal social structure (which characterizes most of India including Tamil Nadu) of the colonial period, and earlier, prevades almost every sphere of social activity. The reality of democratic processes, such as community participation in social decision-making, has yet to materialize in the Indian context. Yet, we make a plea on pragmatic grounds, that government agencies sincerely seek input from the community, at least in their own self-interests, to ensure that projects are successful. In the long-term, it is not in the interest of the bureaucracy to implement *unsuccessful projects* which waste public resources. There is bound to be some political backlash if such wastage occurs. Thus, the time and effort required for consultation with the community may have long-term benefits for the implementing agency as well.

It is also very important for the facilitators and promotors of the projects to be socially and culturally similar to the population with which they are working. It is the responsibility of the promoters to provide information (as health educators), and at the same time to solicit the views of the recipients regarding their needs for sanitation, such as privacy, modern conveniences, etc. Social pressures in terms of enforcement can be achieved if a decision is taken through *consensus,* particularly involving the village/town leaders. However, some effort must be taken to involve a large cross-section of people, not just the leaders if the project is to succeed.

Institutional Aspects

The implementation of a sanitation programme is essentially a strategy of "directed social change", in that the values, attitudes and behaviours of the target groups have to undergo change. This cannot occur automatically by the government fiat. The government agency must act as a *change agent* who must create and manage the technical and social institutions necessary for implementation. The *establishment of effective institution happens to be the essential instrumental problem of delivering technology.*

An institution can be described as "a change-inducing and change-protecting formal organization". Thus, institution-building involves the planning, structuring and guidance of new or reconstituted organizations which can effect changes in values, functions, physical and/or social technologies.

What does this mean for a low-cost sanitation programme? The adoption of various sanitation technologies can occur only if there are viable institutions for *delivering the technology.* Delivery does not mean building toilets of different designs.

Delivery of technology requires participation of the community in decision-making, planning, implementation, maintenance and monitoring. Self-help strategies can be employed wherever possible. It also requires providing environmental health education to the community. It is necessary to influence the community by persuasive communication methods, and by developing innovative strategies for behaviour modification. Thus, the government agency must be able to convince the community of the environmental health benefits resulting from the introduction of sanitation technologies, and, also obtain the involvement of the community in introducing these technologies.

Clearly, these goals can be achieved only if the agency has adequate resources — financial and human, the competence and the support of the larger political and administrative apparatus at the State level. Most important is a clear policy directive that sanitation is an important goal of development, and that resources will continue to be provided to implement the programme.

Thus, the institution must have the capacity to:

(a) adapt to various environmental and socio-economic conditions;
(b) deal with complexity both in terms of technical options and social structures;
(c) be autonomous in implementing the programmes; and
(d) enunciate a coherent long-term strategy that is tied to development.

We conclude this paper with the following policy recommendations:

Policy Recommendations

These recommendations are based on the arguments in this paper and along the lines suggested by the World Bank Studies in Sanitation.

First, the socio-economic base for feasibility planning must be improved. Security of tenure may be necessary for the recipients to agree to share in the cost of the project. Income, social status, or other groupings may affect the demand for various sanitation technologies. Values and attitudes are clearly factors affecting demand, which may have to be altered. An attempt must be made to provide the community with various low-cost technologies, and allow them to choose that technology which is cost effective and suitable for their environment. To repeat, a community cannot be forced into accepting a technology that they do not want.

Secondly, the promoters must provide *incentives.* People do not change their behaviour unless there is some incentive to change, such as financial subsidies. This is not an argument for providing free services. The recipients will value the service less if it is free. Also the Government agencies lose valuable resources which can be used for construction elsewhere. The recipients must be encouraged to share in the maintenance of the facility either by cost-sharing or by their labour (self-help).

Thirdly, the Government must guarantee *continuity* of the strategy. Neither agencies nor communities will make commitments and undertake construction if clear evidence of consistent support is not there. Also, frequent reassessment of the technology is necessary to understand suitability to environmental conditions, acceptance by communities, etc.

Lastly, the Government must provide competent *staffing* to undertake long-term development programmes. The staff must be provided with proper training not only on the technological aspects, but also on the various social and economic factors that preclude acceptance. They must understand their role as "change agents", not merely service providers. A fair degree of autonomy has to be provided to ensure that they can perform this role successfully. They must also be provided with adequate career opportunities so that they do not become frustrated.

Thus, a programme for low-cost sanitation must not be planned and implemented solely in terms of the available technological options. While the technology must be functional and perform adequately in the field, its introduction is beset by a whole range of economic, social and institutional factors. The thrust of this paper is a plea for the Government to take stock of these factors, provide adequate resources, pledge long-term commitment to the goals of the programme; and most importantly involve the community in implementation. It is our judgement that any programme which does not meet these basic requirements will be unsuccessful, and will also be detrimental to the future development of Tamil Nadu.

19

LOW COST SANITATION PROJECT IN TAMIL NADU : Social Aspects

N. ATHIMOOLAM

Out of 728 urban towns in Tamil Nadu, excluding the Madras metropolitan area, sewerage facilities are in operation in 16 towns and sewerage schemes are under execution in seven towns. Hence for the balance 705 towns, sewerage facilities are yet to be provided. Under the Sixth Plan, a provision of Rs. 11.78 crores for sewerage schemes and Rs. 3 crores for low-cost sanitation schemes has been made. Under the Seventh Plan, provision of Rs. 15.411 crores for sewerage schemes and Rs. 7.09 crores for low-cost sanitation schemes has been made. The TWAD Board is at present executing the Low Cost Sanitation Programme in 14 Municipalities with World Bank Assistance.

The Low Cost Sanitation project is programmed to be carried out in two stages. Under Stage I, all the existing dry or bucket latrines will be converted into pour-flush water-seal latrines with a few numbers of new construction. A few community latrines will also be converted or renovated from bucket or dry type into pour-flush latrines under Stage I. The total population coverage will be about 47 per cent of the 1971 population (i.e. 2,36,365 out of 5,02,903) under Stage I and which is included in the World Bank Project. The balance has to be taken up at II Stage.

The total cost of the project under Stage I is Rs. 7.0955 crores with World Bank aid on loan basis. Out of the total number of 29,807 latrines, 10,299 were completed by March 31, 1988. During 1988-89, it was proposed to construct 12,500 of which 3,600 were completed by August 31, 1988. The project was completed in 1989-90.

Implementation of the programme is being done by the TWAD

Board. However inviting applications from the public for constructing the latrines in individual houses, processing of application of individual house owners, watching and effecting recoveries from the house owners, and repayment to the Government for the loan sanctioned are the responsibility of the concerned local bodies.

A "Low Cost Sanitation Cell" has been established with the Director of Municipal Administration, and the Managing Director, TWAD Board, as members to assist in coordinating and promoting related project activities such as Health, Education, etc.

Financing Pattern

Based on the availability of the three basic utilities in the family, namely (1) electricity, (2) water connection and (3) dry latrines, the loan amount of 100 per cent, 50 per cent and 25 per cent of the cost of each unit is given to the individual household. The balance is treated as grant. The financing pattern would be as under.

Category Household latrines	Access to utilities	Loan/Grant (percentage)
I	2 or 3	100/0
II	One only	50/50
III	None	25/75
Community latrines	Impracticability of construction of individual household latrines	0/100

There are various constraints that stand in the way of providing sewerage and sewage treatment systems in the urban and semi-urban areas in India. The only alternative to overcome this is to go in for the low-cost sanitation schemes by conversion of dry latrines into sanitary latrines and construction of new flush latrines wherever no household latrine is available, which can be considered as an appropriate and immediate arrangement to have a safe disposal of highly pathogenic waste to suit the local conditions. The main constraints in implementation of the elaborate sewerage and sewage treatment systems are finance and time. Social aspects are also involved in this conversion programme of provision of sanitary latrines and is being dealt with in this paper.

Evaluation Studies of Ongoing Programmes

Evaluation of the ongoing latrine conversion/construction programmes in the three States of Bihar, Gujarat and Tamil Nadu were carried out by three independent organizations financed by the Technology Advisory Group (TAG) to assess the reactions of the adopters and non-adopters of different socio-economic status, in varying geological and hydrogeological conditions towards the pour-flush water-seal latrines and to identify the constraints in the implementation of the programme and their remedial measures.

The study had the objectives to:

- study the nature and extent of unemployment problem that would be faced by the existing scavenger labour.
- assess the response or reaction of the scavengers, particularly those who have customary rights and
- suggest measures for the economic rehabilitation of the scavengers as a consequence of mass-scale implementation of this programme.

The findings relating to social aspects only are discussed below:

1. The most significant finding of this study is that the latrine conversion programme has neither created unemployment nor underemployment among the scavengers, because of the larger new employment avenues available. Even after the conversion of dry latrines, many houscholders continue to employ scavengers to clean their flush latrines and courtyards and also collect daily garbage. Thus the scavengers need not handle or come in contact with the night-soil at all. Further cleaning of the leach pits of the water-seal latrines, construction of new houses in ever forming housing and other colonies in all the urban areas have forced the local bodies to employ more sweepers and other sanitary workers. The scope of sanitary workers' employment has also increased due to their employment in educational institutions, commercial organisations, financial institutions, head offices of the public and private sectors.
2. Majority of the householders who are without latrines or are with dry latrines are aware of the availability of water-flush

latrines and their advantages. They are really not satisfied with their present dry latrines or open defecation practices. The conversion programmes of dry latrines is popular amongst every section of the public, irrespective of caste, community, religion and occupation.

3. The "adopters" as well as "non-adopters" prefer the ceramic pan with traps instead of mossaic or cement concrete ones even though the ceramic pans are somewhat costlier. People have shown preference for twin-leach pit system against the prevalent single-pit system.

Exclusive use of an independent latrine for each household is preferred among the adopters in spite of their poor economic condition. Most of the "non-adopters" do not like to go in for a common "pour-flush" water-seal latrine to be shared with others and they prefer to continue their present unhygienic practice of use of dry latrine or open defecation.

Majority of the adopters feel that the technical guidance provided particularly in the operation and maintenance of pour-flush latrines and its leach pit was not adequate.

There is a general misconception and apprehension to a lesser extent about the water-seal latrines among the non-adopters, about the high cost, pit collapse, bad smell, effective fixtures etc.

Both the adopters and non-adopters are strongly of the view that the existing formalities of the programme are too complicated and time-consuming.

Vigilance or monitoring service during construction, as also for looking into the grievances of adopters without any delay, personal inspection in the first fortnight of completion of construction to find out any problems and also to educate the householders about proper "up-keep" of the units are found wanting and considered necessary.

Maximum response was available where full funds were available for construction without the householder having to contribute any money before the start of the construction.

Given a choice, people prefer subsidy to a loan. But individual involvement is essential for the success of the project. Most people are ready for adoption of the programme, if long-term government loans with easy instalments of repayment are made available.

The local bodies should therefore evolve a method for recovery of the loan so that the weaker sections of society may not have to pay more than 2 per cent of the income monthly towards the repayment of the loan taken by them. This can however be subject to a minimum (say) of Rs. 20 which they would be incurring, if the scavenger system is to continue.

Development of a "new-felt" need for a better defecation facility, operation of legal sanctions for implementation of the scheme and growing dissatisfaction with the deteriorating latrine-cleaning services have been the three most potent factors behind adoption by a majority of the people.

Satisfied adopters are the best promoters and dissatisfied adopters are the greatest detractors.

The latrine conversion programme is beneficial to the scavenger community as follows:

1. The scavengers are saved from carrying or handling the night-soil.
2. Scavengers are not adversely affected economically because their income had in fact increased due to other areas of work such as cleaning the flush-out latrine, etc., in each household.
3. Change of pollutable occupation had been an inevitable avenue for raising social status of the scavengers. Their status has improved within their own caste, though in relationship to other castes, they continue to suffer the opprobrium and the disabilities of their caste status even after giving up virtually their unclean occupation. But this is bound to be erased over a period of time with simultaneous other development activities for these lower status people.
4. The change of occupation has not resulted in any geographical mobility in most cases (i.e. no migratory resultant has come).
5. Change of occupation has affected the life-style of one-third of the scavengers.
6. Change of occupation has also favourably raised the self-respect, temperament and habits of most scavengers.
7. It also provided them more leisure and more time for others work.
8. It has prevented diseases which is an effective method to control and raise the public health standards of society.
9. A large number of scavengers supported their children who did not want to undertake scavenging work.

Community Latrines

Since in each project town, there would be some households which cannot be provided with individual sanitary latrines due to space constraints, apart from some homeless and floating population, community latrines will have to be resorted to, to a limited extent in each project town but they should be operated and maintained to give a reasonably good and satisfactory service.

These can be located near bus stands, railway stations, market areas, educational institutions which are mostly used by commuters, low-level daily-wage workers, unorganized sector workers, and floating population.

Community latrine programme is satisfactorily maintained only at places where the units are auctioned by the local bodies and manned by private agencies. Pay-and-use type latrines have become popular in many States.

Prominent reasons for the non-use of the community latrines are lack of cleanliness, cost factor, overcrowding, ignorance of its merits and distance from their place. Women can use it, only if separate seats and women attendants are provided. Also overhead tanks of adequate storage capacity with 24-hours water supply should be made available. Proper lighting arrangement inside the latrines is also necessary.

Conclusions

For the low-cost sanitation programmes to be successful, sociological problems will have to be given due attention and ways and means to solve them found.

20

SOCIOLOGICAL APPROACH TO EVALUATION OF COMMUNITY TOILET COMPLEXES

SACHCHIDANANDA

Evaluation plays a very positive role in the development process currently going in the developing countries. Resources being scarce, in terms of both finance and manpower, as also organization, the real problem is to achieve optimum results avoiding possible wastage and linkage in the implementation of the programme for social and economic development of which we had no prior knowledge or expertise. Evaluation spreads that consciousness, builds an ·nvironment and public pressure which alerts both the policy-makers and the planners to organize the whole planning exercise in a more meaningful way.

The term 'evaluation' denotes a series of measurements made of a project for purposes of description, comparison, analysis, comprehension and explanation. The task of evaluation is first to describe then to analyse and finally to seek explanation of the situation. If evaluation is not to remain a sterile exercise confined to description, but is to become in its turn a means of impinging on the evolution of the project, the evaluator must proceed to the more complex task of comparing and analysing the results obtained during the initial descriptive stage. Thus, the first two stages of the process of evaluation lead to the third stage which is designed to enable the evaluator to understand and comprehend what is happening. This stage makes for evaluation for purposes of comprehension and explanation. Evaluation work of this kind necessitates the handling of delicate instruments as the utilization of sophisticated techniques and consequently requires highly competent personnel.

Before taking up a project we have to ascertain whether the socio-psychological climate has been created for its acceptance. It is also to be seen whether the persons who are running the project are adequately trained for their job and also how to make the individuals concerned to become more active agents in the process of socio-economic development. Thus, the major tasks of an evaluation unit might comprise project feasibility studies, research aimed at identification of programme content, evaluation of quantitative results obtained from the systems, evaluation of the attainments in terms of cultural, social, economic, technical and other transformations and actual predictive changes.

Experimental projects should be particularly searching in scrutiny. Their planning will of necessity be highly complex. It is essential to plan the majority of the experiments envisaged before the programme of training is launched. The evaluation of an operational project comprises first and foremost a system of controls making it possible to determine in the most impartial manner possible whether the quantitative objective assigned at the outset have been attained and by means of scientific measurement to identify the factors which militate in favour of or in position to the action for the project.

Irrespective of whether the project to be evaluated is experimental or operational, a distinction has to be made between external and internal evaluation. External evaluation involves the comparison of actual results achieved by the programme with its assigned objectives within a specific framework (financial, geographic, human, etc.). Such evaluation is best carried out by specialized agencies unconnected with the project. Internal evaluation, on the other hand, may be attempted through the project personnel itself. It may not be attempted only after the completion of the project but for midstream adjustment or correction. Such evaluation can lead to feedback intervention. Internal evaluation will thus be concerned with programme content and presentation, programme organization, the training programme, etc.

Of late, many projects have gained immensely through participatory evaluation. In this the beneficiaries of the programme participate in the evaluation process. Since the programme is expected to benefit a number of people in a particular locality, it would be advantageous to take them into confidence from the very beginning. Their participation at the planning and implementation stage will pay rich dividends. In case this was not done earlier their participation at the evaluation stage will be extremely useful. Since these people have a stake in the programme, their interest will make them consider all aspects. The evaluation will thus be very practical and earthy.

Community toilet complexes are extremely necessary both in rural and urban areas. In most of the urban slums the dwellings have no provision for toilet and men, women and children have to ease themselves somewhere. While children ease themselves on the roadside, men and women have to go some distance from their houses in the early hours of the morning or after dark to attend to the call of nature. Besides this, in large towns there is a study in flow and outflow of commuters and pavement dwellers. For such sections of the population, it is further necessary to put up community toilet complexes. This will help in preserving clean environment and save people from going long distances. While putting up these complexes it is necessary to choose such sites where a large number of people congregate. Some of these complexes may be put in slum areas. It has been seen that the users of these facilities do not mind token payment which they have to make for this purpose. From time to time, the literate or articulate users may be asked to complete some schedule in the local language, so that their reactions to these facilities and suggestions for their improvement may be known. In the rural areas particularly, in parts of the village inhabited by the Scheduled Castes, such complexes may be put up. In the localities inhabited by the backward sections of the population community complexes for women may be put up. In fact, with the new powers being given to the Panchayats all over the country, this may be one of the priority areas of action. This will give some satisfaction to women as it will answer a long-felt need. In residential schools in rural area the community toilet complexes may also be used for given electrical power for lighting as well as cooking in the hostels.

The idea of having rural and urban community toilet complexes as conceived by Dr. Bindeshwar Pathak has paid rich dividends not only in this country but abroad. It is, therefore, necessary to expand the programme to many more areas in the country.

If the areas in which these complexes have been functioning for a long time an evaluation should be made of their impact, not only of the sanitation of the area but of the general socio-economic development, their attitude of life and to the application of technology for the solution of their other day-to-day problems. I feel that changes in this sphere would naturally affect the entire thinking process of individuals, their attitude to change and their worldview.

21

LOW COST SANITATION : Organization, Training and Extension

A.K. LAL

Low cost sanitation represents an important innovation capable of solving the major sanitary problems of the developing nations. There is however a strong need for its widespread acceptance among the people. Till recently the attempts in this regard have been by and large casual as well as sporadic. Sustained efforts for its wider diffusion have been lacking. As a consequence attempts thus far made could touch only the fringe of the problems as most of them remained confined to altering the cognitive orientation of the people. The designs developed did not get proper communication for needed interest articulation or acceptance among the people. These also failed to catch the imagination of the people on account of the inherent limitations. With the advent of the Sulabh Shauchalaya, however, a major break-through seems to have been ushered. Under the leadership of Dr. Bindeshwar Pathak a voluntary organization named Sulabh Shauchalaya Sansthan developed a highly workable and effective design of low-cost latrine for its acceptance among the people.

The Sulabh Shauchalaya is a safe and economical alternative to the sewerage and septic tank for disposal of night soil. The technology is intermediate between the highly sophisticated on the one hand and primitive and obsolete on the other. It is compatible with nature. It is a small-scale enterprise which is cheap, locally manageable, efficient and fulfils the conditions for being modern and scientific. It puts a heavy premium on smallness and is self-sufficient. It is not at all complex, it is rather convenient and manageable. It is not large-scale, centralized and resource extensive. It ensures maximization of the benefit from the limited available resources. In fact its simplicity and smallness make it appropriate to meet the local needs. It is a technology that is appropriate to the particular situation faced by the people of the developing nations. Satisfaction of the basic human needs through locally available materials and local labour supplies are its broad objectives. The technology is appropriate on economic and factor endowment grounds. It is a low-profile innovation used as foundation for a wider action frame. It marks a technological leap in the field of sanitation to tackle some of our basic problems. Its relevance transgresses the boundaries of States and regions. In fact the interest that it has evinced is transnational in character. In a way it represents the latest most important means for improving the quality of living.

The diffusion of this low-cost technology for excreta disposal has led to a departure in a situation characterized by inertia, inaction and confusion. It has helped emergence of a rounded perspective for the solution of scientific sanitary problems. Capable to meet a long neglected technological choice, it has ushered a successful and radical departure from the past. The Sulabh Shauchalaya represents a continuous change promising large-scale environmental modifications.

Till this day we have failed to locate even a single active or passive rejector to the scheme. Large-scale adoption of the Sulabh Shauchalaya indicates the fulfilment of the latent desires for change among the people. The innovation has found a permanent stay in the society. It is also evident that the social structure on which the innovation has been grafted is highly supportive. There is no relationship between degree of urbanity and extent of adoption of the scheme. Its spread is not defined to any particular milieu. Acceptance has been accorded on account of its potentiality to remove the incongruity between prevalence of the primitive on the one hand and the urge for novelty on the other. The element of inevitability, orientation to immediate gratification, transparent efficiency, simplicity of the scheme, appropriateness to the culture and relative advantage over the replaced are some of the factors that account for greater degree of acceptance. In a way it also represents the latest and most important means for improvement of quality of life. In fact the changes ushered both in the quantity and in the quality of man's environment improvement have produced a new situation. As a result of this scheme certain changes are discernible in patterns of behaviour and orientations of the impact group. The values transmitted have come to stay with the people. These have become the part of their own. The mental make-up has changed.

The programmes of the Sulabh Shauchalaya has led to a planned institutional change to bring about a better fit between human needs and aspirations on the one hand and the social policy and programmes on the other. Its success in liberating thousands of scavengers from the job of carrying night soil is compatible with human value and egalitarian ethic. Scavenging is an occupation that exhibits a large degree of occupational inheritance and low degree of mobility. Caste identification is directly related to occupational identification. There are instances where the Scheduled Castes have imbibed Sanskritik values to claim a change in their status. Social cohesion for mobility through the political mobilization has been reported to be the phenomenon in a few cases. These have had very limited contributions in achieving the goal of elevated social status for these people. The repatterning of the occupational structure accompanying the urbanization have not helped those who are at the rock bottom of the caste hierarchy. With the implementation of the scheme of construction of Sulabh Shauchalaya leading to the liberation of scavengers, there has been disjunction of occupation from caste so far as these people are concerned. The programme thus has the credibility of having struck for the first time at the foundation of the old social structure in the most significant manner.

Innovations do not necessarily reach people on their own. They have to be taken to the people. It is only then that they are subjected to trial for subsequent adoption or rejection. This entails an effective demonstration of the innovation seeking acceptance among the people. The conduit to transmit the intent, design and effects of the innovation has therefore to be highly reliable. Thus the role of the change agent that mediates between the sponsoring agency on the one hand and the beneficiaries on the other, acquires a place of importance. He is a major variable to affect the process of diffusion and adoption. His orientation and skill to act properly as a transmission belt require his proper training.

Increasing adoption of low-cost sanitation scheme has been rightly attributed to the appropriateness of the emerging paradigm of sanitation represented by the Sulabh Shauchalaya. It is at the same time also reflective of the effectiveness of the change agent which in turn is the measure of the training they have been subjected to. Training for skilful performance has emerged as a permanent concern of the Sulabh International. We have a centre exclusively devoted to the task of imparting training. Training has acquired a central place in Sulabh. It is highly functional. It is our conviction that training helps in making an organization effective in the delivery of goods and services. Internal strategy of the institute puts a heavy premium on combining the various discrete resources into purposeful inputs. It goes on to relate those inputs in proper quantities and sequences, so that they make up a training programme that achieves real impact. During the training the social worker is exposed to learning opportunities from which he identifies the priority themes for internalization. He is also subjected to encounter the practical situation. Proper guidance and expert feedback lead to stamping in of the technological skills and behavioural pattern conducive to the promotion of the goals to which the organization is dedicated. During the training period an attempt is made to rid the habits and thoughts that are ingrained. This is followed by training for preparation of taking up new status and performing new roles not found to be present in him as a component of his habitual behaviour. New orientations are helped to emerge and behavioural pattern oriented to the growth of social entrepreneurship for social interventions are fostered. To transmit content and provide increasing conceptual understanding resort is made to academic strategy. This is accompanied or followed by activity strategy which emphasizes practice of a particular skill. For widening and deepening participants' competence, so as to understand and deal with any situation, resort is made to personal development strategy. Desired inputs for development are acquired through the training at the centre. He in turn helps percolation of contents acquired to the potentates, opinion leaders, lay people either himself or through his counterparts at different cutting edges.

It is our conviction that promotion of a low-cost sanitation scheme requires a comprehensive training programme. In the first place change agents are to be trained in the technological skills and desired behavioural pattern for ensuring wider acceptance of a sanitary programme among the people. At the same time attempts to prepare a fertile ground for the spread of such technology are to be made through mass awareness programmes at different levels of society. Concerned government functionaries have to be made aware of the urgency and social necessity for implementation of the programme. Willing acceptors and supportive bureaucrats can provide an ideal situation for the desired dissemination of the programme contents. With this aim in view the training centre of the Sulabh International has launched either on its own or in collaboration with national and international agencies, programmes for interest articulation and construction and maintenance of low-cost latrines. The impact has been a favour of emergence of sanitation culture in India poised to get entrenched in the years to come. Sanitation is not an insular concept. It has the potentiality of being better accepted if integrated with the wider strategies of development. This realization has led to launching of a massive programme for rural development and self-employment. To widen and deepen the worker's competence to understand and deal with any situation the personal development strategy of training has been resorted to. We are running courses for orientating people for social work in the field of social work, providing needed training inputs to State functionaries entrusted with the task of executing training programmes, helping evolution of Sulabh community centres manual social workers to help people through their knowledge of paramedics, social forestry, sinking and maintenance of drinking water pumps, construction and maintenance of low-cost latrines, bio-gas plants and smokeless *chulhas*. An ambitious project to train 25,000 unemployed youths submitted by us is under the active consideration of the Planning Commission. In addition we have been providing training for acquisition of masonry skills to help raise the status of women working as casual labourers. Engineers and masons have also availed themselves of our facilities for acquisition of the necessary know-how for the construction of low-cost latrine.

On the basis of our experience we have been in a position to locate some important guidelines to orient training programme on low-cost sanitation. These are listed below:

1. Training of change agents does not seem to have received sufficient attention in the earlier efforts for promoting low-cost sanitation.
2. More and more sanitary experts are therefore to be associated to help sanitation training acquire a professional status.
3. Training has to be a continuous process. It has to be a two-way traffic.
4. Training has not to be treated as a feudal wife or a call girl rather a modern housewife.
5. In organizing training institutions having experience of execution have to be an important partner. In experienced theoreticians and ignorant functionaries may not be of much help in the training programme.

6. Training should have a multi-layer and heterogeneous target group.
7. Academic strategy can at best acquire a surrogate status so far as conduct of the training is concerned. Classroom based instructions alone are not enough. Heavy premium is to be placed upon participatory methods.
8. Training should help building an effective communication system to hasten the process of modernization by integrating important contact points in the action-sets activated to achieve targets of development.
9. Distinguishing profiles of the milieu, magnitude of the problem and probable areas of resistance have to be articulated properly in any training programme for diffusion of low-cost sanitation.
10. The social scientist's help in identifying intended and unintended consequences of the change inducted for tackling the available aberrations through modification of the training programmes has to be obtained.
11. Multiple skill inculcation contributes significantly for rounded development.
12. There should be a national policy for effective training for developing a culture of sanitation with its linkages at different points in the country.